GARDEN SPICE
AND
WILD POT-HERBS

GARDEN SPICE AND WILD POT-HERBS

AN AMERICAN HERBAL

by WALTER CONRAD MUENSCHER
Professor of Botany at Cornell University

& MYRON ARTHUR RICE
Horticultural Authority

With illustrations cut on wood by
ELFRIEDE ABBE

Cornell Paperbacks
COMSTOCK PUBLISHING ASSOCIATES
A division of
CORNELL UNIVERSITY PRESS
ITHACA AND LONDON

Published in the United Kingdom by Cornell University Press Ltd., 2-4 Brook Street, London W1Y 1AA.

Limited edition of 90 copies published February 1955.
Popular edition published October 1955.
Second printing January 1956.
First printing, Cornell Paperbacks, 1978.

Library of Congress Cataloging in Publication Data
(For library cataloging purposes only)

Muenscher, Walter Conrad Leopold, 1891-1963.
  Garden spice and wild pot-herbs.

  (Cornell paperbacks)
  Includes index.
  1. Herbs. 2. Herb gardening. 3. Cookery (Herbs) 4. Wild plants, Edible—United States. I. Rice, Myron Arthur, 1897-   joint author. II. Title.
SB351.H5M83 1978   635′.7   78-56899
ISBN 0-8014-9174-6

PREFACE

❡ My curiosity about herbs goes back to 1898, to the time when my mother used to keep a pressed leaf as a book-mark in her Bible. She called the leaf Bibel Blatt. For many years it was known to me only by that name; I had never seen a plant with any flowers to reveal its botanical identity. When at last I saw this same plant in bloom by a roadside in northern New York, the small yellow flower-heads told me at once that the Bible Leaf of my childhood days was the old-fashioned herb, costmary. Thirty-five years ago, when I was a graduate student, my professor came to me with the question, "Do you know anything about herbs?" and asked me to name a plant that had been sent for identification. Ever since that time I have received yearly many letters about herbs. Most of them are requests for identification & inquiries concerning sources of seeds & plants. For twenty-five years I have grown herbs in my garden, acquiring & studying new specimens, and distributing seeds & plants to others who are interested.

In much of the information published on herbs, emphasis has been placed on the historical & legendary aspects; recipes and medicinal uses have been thoroughly treated; but herb literature frequently reveals a lack of accurate botanical information about the plants themselves. This is partly because many herb writers & enthusiasts have had little or no scientific training. Unfortunately, many inaccuracies are reflected in catalogs and advertisements. It is a frequent complaint of gardeners that seed they buy under a certain name proves, on germinating, to be seed of some other plant. Sometimes the same plant is sold under several different names, and the purchaser finds he has bought a duplicate instead of a new kind for his collection. Celery may be sold for lovage, meadow rue for garden rue, American pennyroyal for English pennyroyal; a wider acquaintance with the scientific names, based on ac-

v

curate descriptions of the herbs, would clear up such problems. It is also true that many valuable herbs are not sufficiently known so that more people might enjoy them. This also applies to the wild edible plants treated in Part III of this book. They are of excellent flavor, well-stored with vitamins, and most of them are near at hand for gathering, but through a lack of familiarity with them, people who would appreciate their virtues pass them by.

Part I of this book is devoted to descriptions of the different herbs, principally those employed in cookery; their uses and culture are briefly treated. They are arranged by families, in order to familiarize the reader with the characteristics of each group of herbs & to give him an idea of the relationships of the different kinds. Part II deals with propagation, harvesting, & subsequent treatment. Wild pot-herbs are treated in Part III. Part IV is a brief explanation of the classification and naming of plants in botanical study. Botanical terms are employed to a large extent in the descriptions, since they permit greater accuracy in the necessarily brief statements. The reader may find the glossary helpful. The French, German, and Italian names are given with the description of each herb; they may prove useful to persons more familiar with herbs under their foreign names.

In the illustrations, each plant is shown at natural size unless otherwise noted on the plate. In the case of enlarged figures, such as the mint flowers, the degree of enlargement is indicated immediately below the illustration.

If this book helps to spread more accurate botanical knowledge of the herbs among home gardeners & amateur growers and helps to bring more people good eating, it shall have accomplished its purpose.

W. C. MUENSCHER

Ithaca, New York
May, 1953

Note to Cornell Paperbacks Edition

The list of synonyms on page 204 has been brought up to date and indicates the scientific names currently preferred by horticulturists.

ACKNOWLEDGEMENTS

THE authors wish to acknowledge their indebtedness to all those who have coöperated in the preparation of this book, and to express particular appreciation to two members of the Cornell University faculty, Prof. Harlan P. Banks for his steady encouragement & support, & Prof. C. B. Raymond for his helpful interest & the contribution of certain specimens; also to Dr. Babette I. Brown of the University of Rochester for her assistance in the cultivation, harvesting, and trial of the herbs during the preliminary stages of this study. Mr. Victor Lionel Guzman of Lima, Peru, furnished information on the use of coriander and balm. Prof. E. M. Meader of the University of New Hampshire provided information on Korean mint. Miss Margaret M. Stewart assisted in the compilation of the index. Thanks are due the Herb Grower Magazine for permission to quote from "Herb Recollections". Preparation of this book was aided in part by a grant from the Cornell University Faculty Research Grants Committee.

The illustrations in this book were made from the original woodcuts by Elfriede Abbe, except Plates 45, 56, and the cut on page 69, which are from drawings. Nearly all the illustrations are of live plants grown at Ithaca, New York. The artist also designed the book, which was set in Goudy Kennerley Bold & Italic.

CONTENTS

ℂ INTRODUCTION

HERBS,—culinary, household, savory, aromatic, condimental, or sweet garden plants grown for flavoring or seasoning foods, improving the diet, and preparing enjoyable & healthful tea-like beverages have been cultivated and used since ancient times. They are the garden spice plants, and their essential oils give them characteristic flavors and aromas. Some are reputed to have medicinal values and were employed in the medicinal practice of the ancients, by the herbalists of the Middle Ages, & by physicians and domestic practitioners of the more recent past. To a limited extent, herbs are still so used. Although most culinary herbs are of Old World origin, some are indigenous to America & were utilized by the Indians of this continent. Among the herbs considered in this work, *Monarda didyma* and *Monarda fistulosa* are strictly American. *Lippia citriodora* is from South America.

1

Within recent years there has been an increasing interest in culinary herbs among home gardeners and those concerned with dietetics & food preparation. During the Second World War this was accelerated by the greater emphasis placed on gardening, foods, and nutrition & by wartime shortages of some of the imported flavorings & spices. Many botanists, horticulturists, garden enthusiasts, herb specialists, and dietitians have studied & worked with the culinary herbs & have written about them. Newspaper and magazine articles, circulars, pamphlets, & books provide abundant literature on the subject of herbs.

There are many growers of garden herbs who are more interested in their herbs from the ornamental, historical, or romantic viewpoint than from the viewpoint of culinary use. Some of the herbs, even some of the common culinary ones, are exceedingly useful components of an ornamental garden composition, and it is quite feasible to grow the utilitarian herbs along with & among garden flowers & other ornamentals. They may still be used as household spice plants, and such utilization is favored by the fact that only small amounts are usually required in the average home. The culinary herbs usually do not include the ordinary garden vegetables, with a few exceptions, such as parsley & horseradish, but herbs may be grown as a legitimate part of the home vegetable garden, as is often done. Some gardeners prefer to grow herbs in a distinct & separate section of the garden, & of course there are those who emphasize the herbs in particular & are what we may call herb gardeners.

The practical housewife, with her mind focused on the affairs of the kitchen, the preparation and cooking of food, the serving of meals, & the feeding of her family, may wish to have her savory herbs as close to the kitchen door as may be practicable. In the winter time she may even have some of them growing indoors in flower pots or other containers. She is interested in knowing what the various herbs are good for & how each may be used to best advantage. The uses of the culinary herbs, particularly in foods & beverages, are treated in the main body of this work under the separate discussions of the individual species. For more detailed information about the use of herbs in food recipes the housewife should consult the available cookbooks.

A word should be said about those herbs which are most useful for culinary purposes. What are the best culinary herbs? This is a question of opinion and judgment, a matter of individual choice. If one can grow or obtain only a limited number of kinds, it is well to have some idea of their relative merits. Of all the culinary herbs, parsley, that prosaic vegetable, probably takes the lead. Although used mostly as a garnish in this country, in its diverse utility and popular esteem, it stands at the head of the list. After parsley, there are various herbs of better than average value for kitchen garden & household use, but which it is difficult to list in the order of their comparative merit. In this group should be included basil, common thyme, creeping thyme, sage, summer savory, winter savory, sweet marjoram, wild marjoram, spearmint, bergamot mint, apple mint, chives, and balm. It will be noted that all are grown mainly for their leaves and leafy tips; none belongs to the seed-crop group, such as caraway, coriander, dill, and anise. All are easily propagated and grown. If the householder can grow only a very few herbs, parsley, chives, summer savory, basil, & spearmint might constitute the wisest choice. Some people are especially partial to chives, with its mild onion-like flavor, and consider it to be the best of all herbs for seasoning. Others praise the virtues of summer savory, particularly for flavoring meats & for the preparation of a tea. Some prefer thyme & place it first among all the culinary herbs.

That the culinary herbs have real value & utility is unquestionable, considering the extent to which they are used & enjoyed. By improving the flavor of commonly consumed foods, stimulating the appetite & digestive functions, & in some cases relieving alimentary disorders, they contribute their share to better nutrition. They possess some nutritional value themselves in furnishing certain vitamins. The vitamin content of herbs has not yet been thoroughly studied, but it is known that parsley, in the fresh condition, is rich in vitamin C or ascorbic acid. Those

4

classed as pot-herbs, such as sorrel, dock, & good-king-
henry, are undoubtedly excellent suppliers of the A
and B vitamins, as well as of vitamin C, since the
entire substance of the leaves is consumed. Probably
all herb teas or tisanes made from fresh, green, un-
dried material also contain beneficial amounts of vitamin C.

For garden planting, a small collection of six kinds
of herbs might be laid out in a triangle, with the
long side facing south or east to gain the maximum
sunlight. The mint, whatever kind is chosen, should
occupy the back corner because it is taller than the
other plants & may overrun them if not confined.
A few sage plants may be placed in front of the
mint where they may be left undisturbed for many
years. They become small shrubs & may be cut back
in autumn or early spring to 8 inches above ground
level. The front line of the plot may be edged with
a row of chives, which may be cut freely, & their
position may be bounded by a clump of thyme on
each end. The strip between the sage & the chives
should be spaded each spring for the sowing of parsley or other annuals. With whatever type of garden
plan used, the annuals should be confined to the center of the plot & the perennials to the border. In
such a plan, the roots of the perennials need not be
disturbed by preparation of the soil for the annuals.

PLATE 1

Natural size

One third

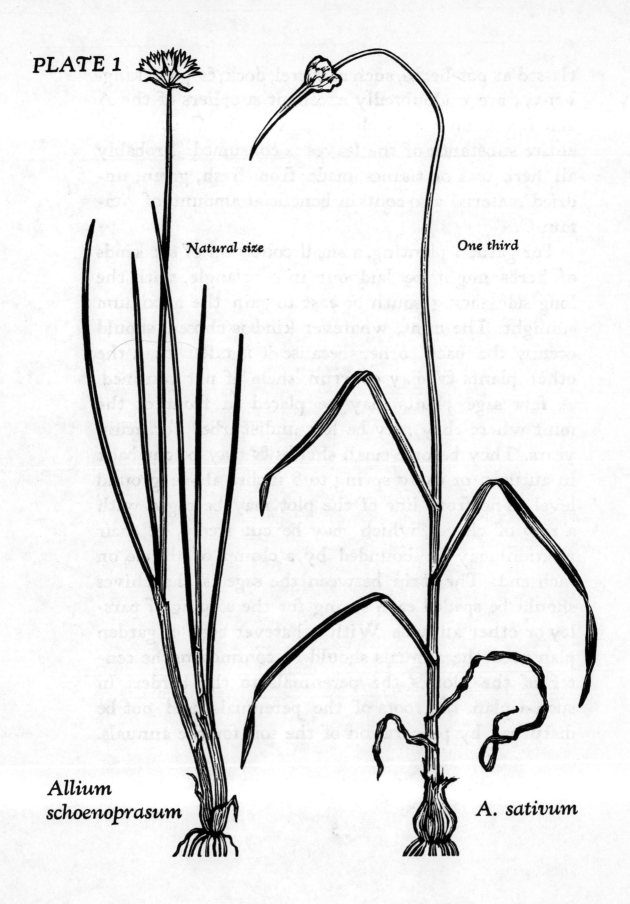

Allium
schoenoprasum

A. sativum

I.

DESCRIPTIONS OF THE HERBS
-ALSO THEIR USE AND CULTURE-

❧

⟨ LILIACEAE ، LILY FAMILY

THIS is a large, important, and well-known family of plants, including at least 2000 species in 200 or more genera, distributed principally in temperate regions. Besides the species of *Lilium*, many other familiar garden flowers belong to this family, such as the tulip, hyacinth, lily-of-the-valley, squill, and colchicum. The flowers are perfect & symmetrical, the perianth typically composed of six parts, either separate or united. The inner and outer parts of the perianth are similar in form and color. The stamens are usually six, the ovary superior & three-celled. The fruit is a few-to-many-seeded capsule or a berry, the capsule loculicidally dehiscent, sometimes indehiscent. The seeds are albuminous. Most of the plants of the Lily Family are herbaceous and perennial, with the exception of a few that tend to be somewhat woody and arborescent.

7

PLATE 2

One third natural size

Allium porrum

*A. cepa
var.
viviparum*

ALLIUM CEPA L. var. VIVIPARUM Metz

Called Top Onion, Tree Onion, & Egyptian Onion.
French: Oignon d'Égypte.

THE TOP onion is usually grown as an annual or biennial. The smooth, glaucous scape grows from 2 to 4 feet high. It is hollow and swollen above the base, as are also the leaves, which do not reach more than half the height of the scape. The flowers, in a terminal umbel, are numerous, white to lilac, the stamens exserted. Bulbels commonly develop in place of flowers & often sprout while still attached to the plant. The underground bulb is not well-developed, usually not becoming much thicker than the stem.

Since the plant does not produce seeds or offsets, the bulbels are used for propagation. They are used in the home kitchen for seasoning & garnishing, and may be pickled according to the following recipe:

Put the bulbels into a pan of wine vinegar with plenty of white peppercorns & cook them for a few minutes; then dip them into a preserve jar, putting in first a layer of tarragon, then a layer of bulbels, next a layer of horseradish, another of bulbels, & so on. When the jar is filled, pour the cooled vinegar over the contents & seal the jar.

The underground bulbs may also be eaten in the same way as "spring onions".

Onions require a rich, well-drained garden loam. The bulbels should be planted as early as possible in

9

spring; they are set 4 inches apart in furrows 1 inch deep & are left uncovered; the furrows should be 1 foot apart. The bulbels are necessarily stored during the winter before planting, & will keep satisfactorily if stored in a cool place.

Plate 2 shows the top onion.

ॐ

ALLIUM PORRUM L. - LEEK

French: Poireau, Porreau.
German: Porree, Winterlauch. Italian: Porro.

THE LEEK is a hardy biennial. The scape has a pithy interior, and in the second year it reaches a height of 2 to 4 feet. The bulb is simple & not much thicker than the stalk. The leaves are keeled & may reach 3 feet in length and 2 inches in width. The large terminal umbel is solitary & compact, several-thousand-flowered, and subtended by a long, acute bract or spathe. The flowers are white, bluish, or pinkish, the stamens exserted, three of them having prolongations on each side of the anther. Cultivated varieties include Broad London or Large American Flag, Prizetaker, & Large Musselburgh.

The stems & leaves, usually blanched, are used to

flavor soups & stews. Cooking dissipates the strong odor & makes the flavor mild & pleasing. Leek may be used as a principal soup ingredient; the ancient Scotch dish, cock-a-leekie, is a chicken soup thickened with leeks. They may be boiled & served like asparagus, also eaten raw, or may be sprinkled with grated cheese & crumbs & browned under the broiler. The bulb has sometimes been employed in medicine as a kidney stimulant.

Propagation is sometimes by bulbs, but usually by seeds, which are started in indoor seed-beds from mid-February to late March. Germination occurs in about ten days in a favorable temperature range from sixty to seventy degrees. When 2 to 4 inches high, the seedlings are thinned to 2 inches apart. They are planted outdoors from early May to early June, being set 6 to 9 inches apart in the rows, which may be from 18 inches to 3 feet apart. Seed may be sown directly outdoors as soon as the ground is workable, one ounce of seed to one hundred feet of row. Depth of planting should be one quarter inch, & the plants should be thinned to stand 4 to 6 inches apart. They are blanched by gradually banking with earth or are grown by the celery trenching method; they are also grown like onions, without bleaching. May-planted leeks are available for use in September; when grown as a second crop to follow early vegetables, the seed is started indoors in April or early May, & the seedlings are planted out in July. If started in coldframes in late August, they may be set out the following spring. Leeks are dug before freezing & stored like celery, the storage period being four to six weeks. The plants are favored by a light, moist, fertile loam.

Of uncertain origin, the leek is said to be native to the Mediterranean region; it grows wild in Algeria. It has been grown & used in Egypt since the most ancient times. See Plate 2.

ALLIUM SATIVUM L. ⸴GARLIC

Also called Clown's Treacle. German: Knoblauch. French: Ail, Perdrix de Gascogne. Italian: Agliotti, Ai.

℀ GARLIC IS A perennial, onion-like plant, but has flat leaves. The scape is alternate-leafy below, not swollen, & the compound bulb is composed of several parts called cloves, bulblets, chives, or beans enclosed in a common papery envelope. The height of the leaves reaches to 12 inches, the scape 36 inches. The small, white to pink flowers are enclosed before e-mergence by a thin-walled, sack-like, long-beaked spathe; bulbels often develop instead of flowers.

Cloves of the bulb are used sparingly for condiment in cookery & sometimes to impart a mere flavor or aroma; they are used in seasoning forcemeats and are incorporated in chutney & marinating mixtures.

They are rubbed on the inside of the salad-bowl or on bread which is added to soups & pot-herbs. Garlic also flavors stews, pot-cheese, cream-cheese, omelettes, pickles, sauces, dressings, vinegar, & sausages such as bologna; it is rubbed on roast beef & lamb before cooking. For garlic vinegar, four to six bruised cloves are used with one quart of vinegar.

Garlic has uses in medicine as an expectorant, diaphoretic, rubifacient, & antiseptic; it is said to stimulate the nerves & circulation and is used in the treatment of bronchitis, coughs, colds, boils, & ulcers. Expressed and diluted, the juice may be applied to wounds & is an ingredient of ointments & lotions. It is used in veterinary medicine as an anthelmintic.

Propagation is by bulbels from the inflorescence and by bulblets or cloves of the bulb. Early spring planting is best in the North, fall planting in the gulf coast section of the South, & planting from November to January in California. Cloves are set 1 to 2 inches deep & 4 to 6 inches apart in rows about 16 inches apart. Fertile, well-drained, sandy loam favors garlic. Bulbs are harvested when the tops begin to turn dry & yellow, are dried for a brief time and stored in a cool, dry, well-ventilated place. In California they are harvested in July or August, in Louisiana in May, farther north in June. They are then plaited by the tops into strings, tied in bunches, or packed in mesh bags & crates. Small cellophane bags of the cloves are sold in stores for home kitchen use.

13

A European plant, cultivated since ancient times, garlic is grown commercially in Louisiana, Texas, Oregon, & California. It is bought & consumed mostly by the Latin population of the larger cities & is used to some extent by restaurants and hotel chefs. It is also esteemed generally in the southwestern United States, especially by Spanish-speaking people.

The leaves are sometimes attacked by onion thrips. Plate 1 shows the plant before flowering.

ALLIUM SCHOENOPRASUM L. , CHIVES

Also called Cives & Chive-Garlic.
French: Civette, Ciboulette, Petit Porreau.
German: Schnittlauch. Italian: Erba Cipollina.

PERENNIAL onion-like plants, chives grow in dense clumps, the cylindrical, hollow leaves reaching a height of about 12 inches, often less. The bulbs are but slightly thicker than the stems and are closely crowded. The attractive lavender flowers are clustered in heads on scapes which do not surpass the leaves in height. The fruit is a small, gray, papery capsule, containing one or more pointed black seeds.

The leaves are used as flavoring, as a pot-herb, and as salad greens. Chopped fresh, they flavor omelettes, scrambled eggs, croquettes, jellied chicken, mashed potatoes, cooked beans, cheeses, sandwich fillings, stews, soups, salads, & hot vegetables; they may be mixed with other sweet herbs. The leaves may also be used dried in most of these dishes & also in fondues. The bulbs are used in sausage and may be pickled like small onions.

Chives make an ornamental edging in the flower garden. Propagation may be by bulbs or seeds but is usually by division of clumps. Plants should be renewed every two to four years. They thrive in average garden soil, especially in full sunlight. When leaves are cut off, new leaves develop. It has been our experience that chives produce seeds in great abundance. The species is native & wild in Europe and Siberia. The cultivated type is reputed to have come from the region of the Alps. See Plate 1, showing variety *sibiricum*, a form with longer scape.

ALLIUM ASCALONICUM L. , SHALLOT

Also called Scallion & Cibol.
French: Échalote, Ciboule. Italian: Scalogno.
German: Schalotte, Eschlauch, Askalonische Zwiebel.

℄ THE SHALLOT is perennial, reaching a height of 12 inches, sometimes more. The leaves are many, awl-shaped, cylindrical & hollow, not as tall as the scape. The elongate, egg-shaped bulb, covered with a purplish or brownish skin, readily separates into angular cloves which remain attached at the base. Flowers are usually not produced but when present are rose-violet in color, numerous, in a globular head.

The delicately-flavored bulb is chopped or sliced thin & sprinkled on salad. Bulbs may be pickled according to the directions given on page 9, but should first be peeled, sprinkled with salt, and allowed to stand overnight before cooking. Shallots are excellent for flavoring gravies, sauces, soups, stews and left-over meat dishes. Shallot vinegar has a characteristic flavor, milder & sweeter than garlic vinegar.

Culture is essentially the same as for garlic, cloves being planted in March or April in good garden soil, and harvested in July or August, after which period the mature bulbs break apart into new cloves. These may be stored for several months.

The shallot grows wild in Asia, supposedly having originated in Syria. It is not commonly known in the United States but sometimes appears in eastern markets. Other kinds of onions are often sold as shallots.

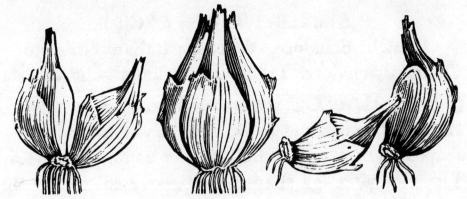

Bulb and cloves of SHALLOT

ALLIUM TUBEROSUM Rottler

Called Garlic-chives & Oriental Garlic.

℄ ORIENTAL GARLIC reaches a height of 12 to 18 inches, the scape surpassing the leaves, which are flat and about a quarter of an inch in width. The erect habit of the plant, the slender leaves & many-flowered umbel suggest the appearance of chives when the plants are seen growing in clumps. The spreading petals & sepals are white with a green central vein. The plants rise from rather slender bulbs which grow on a stout creeping rhizome. Usually not more than four bulbs grow in a cluster.

Culture is similar to that of garlic. *Allium tuberosum* is native and wild in eastern Asia. In Japan and China all parts of the plant are eaten raw, including the flowers which are said to be very good in salad. The flavor of the bulb is somewhat like garlic, but milder. The leaves may be chopped & mixed with cream cheese like chives.

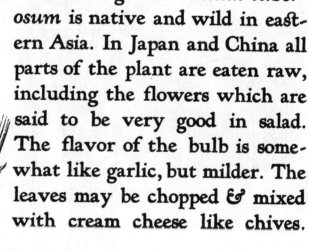

Basal portion of
GARLIC-CHIVES

PLATE 3

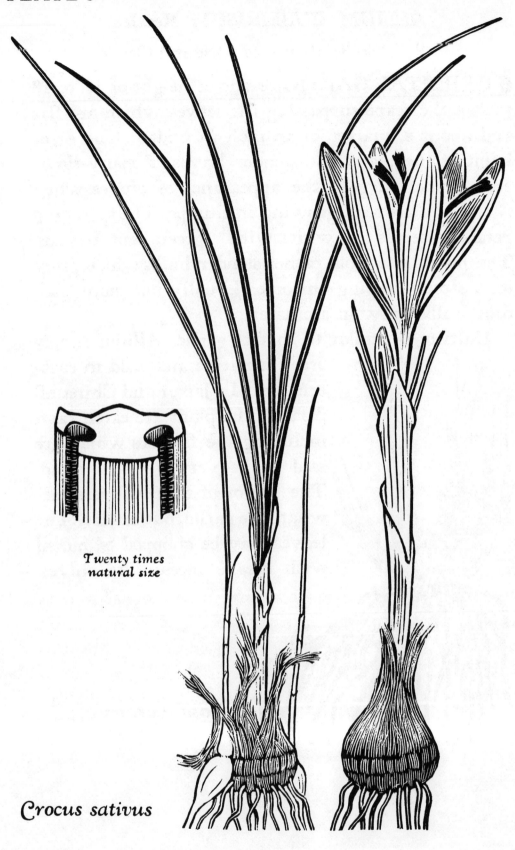

Twenty times
natural size

Crocus sativus

IN ADDITION to the iris, other ornamental members of this family are the gladiolus, the freesia, and the crocus. Most of the plants of the *Iridaceae* are low perennials with unbranched stems, which rise from bulbs, corms, or rhizomes. The leaves are basal and linear. The flowers, which rise from a sheath, are perfect & showy and have three petals, three petal-like sepals, & three stamens alternating with the petals. The ovary is inferior, the pistil solitary with a single style divided in three parts at the apex.

CROCUS SATIVUS L. ˏ SAFFRON CROCUS

French: Safran, Safran d'automne. German: Safran.
Italian: Zafferano, Giallone, Grogo.

The saffron crocus is one of the most commonly cultivated autumn-blooming species. The leaves, rising from a globular corm about an inch in diameter, are linear & sometimes reach a height of 12 inches or more. Their ciliate margins help to distinguish the saffron crocus from other species. A cross-section of a leaf, showing the inrolled ciliate margins, is illustrated in Plate 3. The trumpet-shaped perianth is white to lilac. The stamens have yellow anthers, and the style-branches are red & very prominent. The flowers open only in sunshine. The numerous species of crocus are seldom sold under their scientific names; crocus, moreover, is frequently confused with colchicum, a member of the *Liliaceae*. The latter has six stamens and three distinct styles.

The crocus does well in average soil that is well-drained & free of clay. Corms are planted in September or October & should be set 3 to 4 inches deep and 2 to 3 inches apart for colony formation. They should have a light mulch of straw in northern winters. New corms are freely formed & should be replanted, since they work out of the ground & soon die. No manure should be used in crocus beds.

Crocus sativus is native in Greece & Asia Minor but is no longer found outside of cultivation. It is of very old culture, for saffron was used in ancient Greece, Rome, & the western Orient as a perfume and a dye. The substance, saffron, consists of the dried stigmas of the flowers. It is deep red-orange in color and has an aromatic odor & a hot, pungent taste. Four thousand flowers are required to make an ounce of saffron. An extract was formerly much used in dyes, but it is now replaced by cheaper substitutes. Saffron is sometimes used in the home kitchen to color cake & confectionery or to flavor exotic dishes. In Spain & the Orient it is grown commercially for use as a condiment. Saffron is now much adulterated with safflower. The two names are often confused. Safflower is described in this book under *Compositae*.

ℭ POLYGONACEAE ∘ BUCKWHEAT FAMILY

THE PLANTS of the *Polygonaceae* have ſtems with well-marked nodes or joints, simple leaves, and ſtipules usually united into sheaths at the nodes. Petals are lacking, the perianth consiſting of two to six sepals. The fruit is an angular or winged achene. About thirty genera & seven hundred species are known, the family being represented in moſt parts of the world. Two useful members are buckwheat and rhubarb. Several are common weeds.

RUMEX PATIENTIA L. ∘ DOCK

Also called Spinach Dock, Patience Dock, Passions, Herb Patience, & Monk's Rhubarb.
French: Patience, Oseille-épinard, Épinard Immortel, Parelle. German: Englischer Spinat.

A perennial, dock usually does not bloom before the second year, when the flowering ſtalk may reach 5 feet or more. The erect, sometimes branched ſtem is grooved & glabrous. The basal leaves, including the long petioles, reach a length of at leaſt 12 inches; the blades are ovate-elliptic to ovate-lanceolate, narrowed at the base, the margins wavy; similar but smaller, the upper leaves are more nearly oblong-lanceolate, shorter-petioled to almost sessile, & alter-

21

PLATE 4

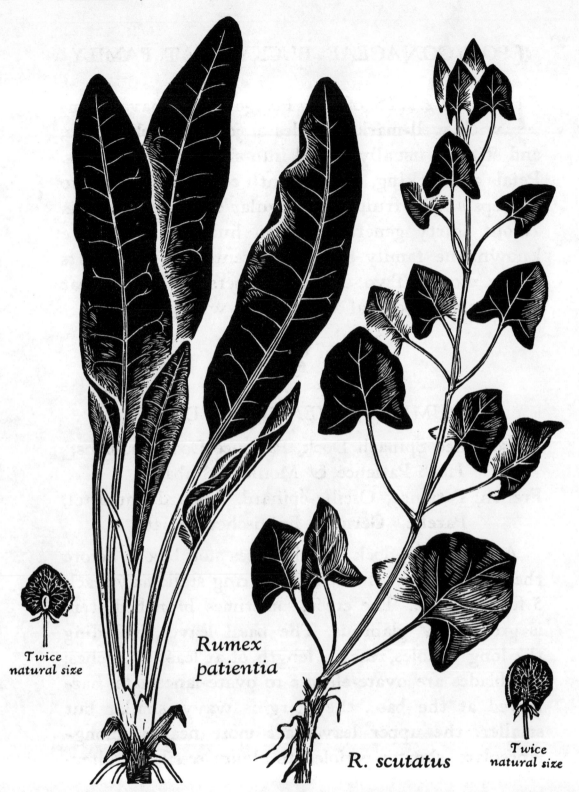

Twice
natural size

Rumex
patientia

R. scutatus

Twice
natural size

nate. The flowers are perfect & are on long, jointed pedicels; they are in whorls which are in compound racemes or panicles, the entire inflorescence reaching 2 or more feet in length. The calyx valves are green, turning brown when mature, entire, cordate at the base, one valve bearing a conspicuous tubercle. The fruit is a brown, shiny, concave-faced achene.

The fresh leaves, rather mild in flavor, are used early in the season as a pot-herb or raw in salad.

Propagation is by seeds, which germinate well and promptly. Dock self-sows & is adapted to rich, moist garden soil & full sun exposure. It is often attacked by a black aphis in mid-season & infected by a fungus which causes a shot-hole disease of the leaves.

Dock is native in Europe & Asia & is naturalized as a wild plant in Newfoundland & southern Canada to Pennsylvania, Kansas, and Wisconsin, and on the Pacific Coast. See Plate 4.

RUMEX SCUTATUS L. ⟋ FRENCH SORREL

French: Oseille ronde, Patience écusson.
German: Schild-ampfer. Italian: Erba Pan a Vin.

⟨ FRENCH SORREL is a perennial, with smooth stems, both prostrate & ascending, the leaves more or less fleshy; the basal ones are long-petioled, cordate-ovate & obtuse, the upper short-petioled, hastatefiddleform, sometimes lobed, acute, & alternate. The calyx-valves surrounding the achene are rounded-cordate, without tubercles. The plant is usually not more than 18 inches in height at maturity.

The leaves are used raw or cooked like dock and garden sorrel (see section III, *Rumex acetosa*), and are good not only in spring but also through midseason. They may flavor sauces, omelettes, & bland greens. The famous sorrel soup of France is made as follows:

Stir a pint of the leaves over the fire until wilted; drain, chop, & put them through a strainer. Put a lump of butter & a sliced onion into a large pot and heat gently. Add the sorrel & a quart of stock, bring to boiling & let simmer for twenty minutes. Stir in a tablespoonful of cornstarch mixed with four table-spoonfuls of milk, add salt & pepper, & pour into a serving dish over the beaten yolk of an egg.

Propagation & culture are much the same as for dock & garden sorrel, but the plants may be spaced farther apart because of their spreading habit.

French sorrel is native in Europe & Asia.

Plate 4 shows a plant before blooming.

ℂ *CHENOPODIACEAE* ⸱ GOOSEFOOT FAMILY

HERBACEOUS, weedy plants are typical of this family. Two useful members are spinach & beet. The leaves are simple, alternate, & without stipules. The flowers are small, greenish, & lack petals. The calyx is persistent, usually enclosing the mature fruit. About five hundred species in seventy-five genera are comprised in the *Chenopodiaceae*. Many of the plants, such as greasewood, grow in desert regions, others in a maritime habitat.

25

ATRIPLEX HORTENSIS L. , ORACH, ARRACH

Butter Leaves, Mountain Spinach, French Spinach.
French: Arroche, Belle-dame, Bonne-dame, Folette.
German: Garten-Melde, Spanischer Spinat.
Italian: Bietolone Rosso.

ⓒ ORACH IS an annual, erect, somewhat branching, with smooth stems & leaves, & grows to a height of 4 feet. The leaves are long-petioled, arrow-shaped or hastate, with wavy to dentate margins, the upper leaves alternate, the lower opposite. The flowers are small & numerous, in racemes clustered in terminal and axillary panicles. There is a kind with red leaves which has ornamental value & is known as variety *atrosanguinea*, sometimes called red spinach; some variations of shade are found in the green form.

Orach is treated as a pot-herb, cooked & served like spinach, & is sometimes combined with sorrel because of its bland flavor. It may be steamed or boiled without much water. The plant is said to be soothing for inflammations, the seeds emetic.

Propagation is by seeds sown in rows 1 to 2 feet apart, the plants thinned 6 to 18 inches apart in the rows. The first early planting may be followed by later plantings every few weeks. The illustration on page 25 shows a plant that has been kept cut back to induce new tender growth. Orach is adapted to a light, well-drained soil & full sun exposure. Watering in dry weather is beneficial. Sometimes Orach

26

PLATE 5

Chenopodium bonus-henricus

self-sows. The related native wild species, *Atriplex patula*, may be similarly used.

Atriplex hortensis is native to central Asia & has been grown as a garden esculent in China & the Mediterranean region since the most ancient times. It is said to have been introduced into Britain in 1548 & grown in America in 1806. It sometimes occurs wild as an escape from cultivation.

CHENOPODIUM BONUS-HENRICUS L.

Called Good-King-Henry, Mercury, Fat Hen, Blite, Wild Spinach, Goosefoot, & Allgood.
French: Bon Henri, Épinard sauvage, Toute-bonne.
German: Guter Heinrich.
Italian: Colubrina, Tuttabuona, Buono Enrico.

GOOD-KING-HENRY is a perennial, usually with several erect, branching stems, reaching 36 inches in height. The leaves are alternate, petioled, triangular-hastate, smooth when mature, with margins entire or slightly sinuate. The flowers are greenish & inconspicuous, in short branched spikes which are terminal and axillary.

The plant is a pot-herb, the leaves being used like spinach; they may also be added to soups. It has been used as a cooling infusion, an alimentary stimulant, and a fomentation on surface inflammations.

Seeds do not germinate well, although plants occasionally volunteer from self-sown seeds. Propagation is usually by division of the roots in spring; the plants are spaced 2 feet apart in rows which should be spaced 2 feet from one another. Plants do well under average garden conditions, in sun or shade, but are favored by partial shade. Not entirely winter-hardy, good-king-henry has nevertheless become a roadside weed from southeastern Canada to southern New York. It originated in Europe.

Plate 5 shows some basal leaves & an inflorescence.

ℭ CRUCIFERAE ˏ MUSTARD FAMILY

A FEW OF THE plants in this family are shrubs; most are herbaceous. Their leaves are usually alternate and simple, but sometimes deeply lobed or compound; stipules are lacking. The flowers consist of four sepals & four petals arranged like a cross, four long & two short stamens, & a solitary pistil. The fruit is a pod which usually splits open by two valves, each containing one or more seeds. Most of the plants have an acrid & pungent juice. Such ornamentals as alyssum, rock cress (Arabis), & candy-tuft belong to the family. Two familiar vegetables are turnip & cabbage. The family consists of two thousand species in two hundred genera, distributed throughout the world.

29

ARMORACIA LAPATHIFOLIA Gilib.
HORSERADISH

French: Cran, Cranson, Moutarde des Allemands,
Moutarde des capucins, Raifort-sauvage.
German: Meerrettich, Kren. Italian: Barba-forte.

HORSERADISH is a perennial, the roots large,
thick, deep, & branching, the flowering stem coarse,
reaching 3 feet in height. The basal leaves have long,
grooved petioles; the blades are at first more or less
pectinate, notched, or fringed, but later oblong-ovate
to oblong, the margins crenate or sinuate, the surface
rough but not hairy. The upper leaves are smaller,
sessile or nearly so, lanceolate, & alternate. The numerous, small, white flowers are in racemes which
are terminal & axillary. The fruit, which is globose
to short-oblong, often fails to mature, and the seeds
are usually non-viable. The sharp flavor & pungent
aroma of the root are due to the glucoside, sinigrin,
which decomposes when the root is grated, scraped,
or ground, liberating a volatile oil similar to that in
mustard seed. The unbroken root is inodorous.

Used as a table relish or in sauce, especially with
fish or fat & salt meats, the root is first washed,
peeled or scraped, & then grated or ground; it is a
favorite condiment with oysters. The grated root,
preserved in distilled or white wine vinegar, is put
up in glass jars for the retail trade & home use. The
fresh whole roots are also sold by food stores & veg-

PLATE 6

*Armoracia
lapathifolia*

One third natural size

etable retailers. The grated root is sometimes soaked in olive oil or other edible oil & is also dried and ground into powder. Horseradish is believed to ameliorate the effects of oily fish & fat meats, stimulate the appetite, & aid digestion. It is sometimes used medicinally as a counter-irritant, like mustard, and is employed by infusion in hot water for the treatment of dyspepsia, scurvy, rheumatism, & hoarseness; one teaspoonful of ground root is used to one cup of boiling water; the infusion is sipped gradually. The fresh root is more pungent than dried or preserved root; the volatile oil liberated by maceration is largely dissipated in drying. Horseradish is also reputed to be stimulant, diuretic, anthelmintic, antiseptic, & in large doses emetic.

For horseradish vinegar, the roots are peeled or scraped & then grated into distilled or white wine vinegar of about five per cent. strength & allowed to steep for a week or more, after which the vinegar is then strained & bottled. Shallots, onions, garlic, or red peppers may be mixed with the grated root before steeping. Horseradish sauce is an alcoholic infusion of the sliced root, used for flavoring white sauce and for the direct flavoring of foods, usually with a little fresh mustard or red pepper.

Plants are propagated by root cuttings. In commercial practice, the side roots are trimmed off in preparing horseradish for the market. Cuttings are 2 to 8 inches in length, the longest best. They are tied in bundles, cool-moist stored until spring, then planted 3 to 4 inches deep and 10 to 15 inches apart, in rows 3 to 4 feet apart, the position of the roots usually slanting. Cuttings are also made by cutting the roots lengthwise into strips 4 to 6 inches long and a quarter of an inch thick; these are planted 12 inches apart, the portion from the large end of the root uppermost. Side roots are rubbed off twice during the growing season to obtain a well formed, acceptable market product. For home use, the roots are usually dug in the fall, stored in cool, moist sand to prevent shriveling, & are used as needed. Horseradish is adapted to rich, moist loam & full sun. For winter salad, fall-dug roots with the crown intact are planted in moist soil in a dark, warm cellar & deeply covered. The leaves that grow out are bleached, tender, and sweet-pungent; they are cut when 3 to 4 inches long and are used alone or in mixed salad.

Horseradish is native in southeastern Europe. It was a medicinal plant of the Middle Ages. It has escaped from cultivation & is naturalized in the United States, where it occurs in low, moist ground, especially along streams, sometimes becoming a troublesome weed. It is grown commercially in New Jersey, Pennsylvania, Massachusetts, Connecticut, Michigan, Ohio, Illinois, & Washington, but the principal producing area is the St. Louis district of Missouri.

The vegetative portions of the horseradish plant are shown in Plate 6.

33

PLATE 7

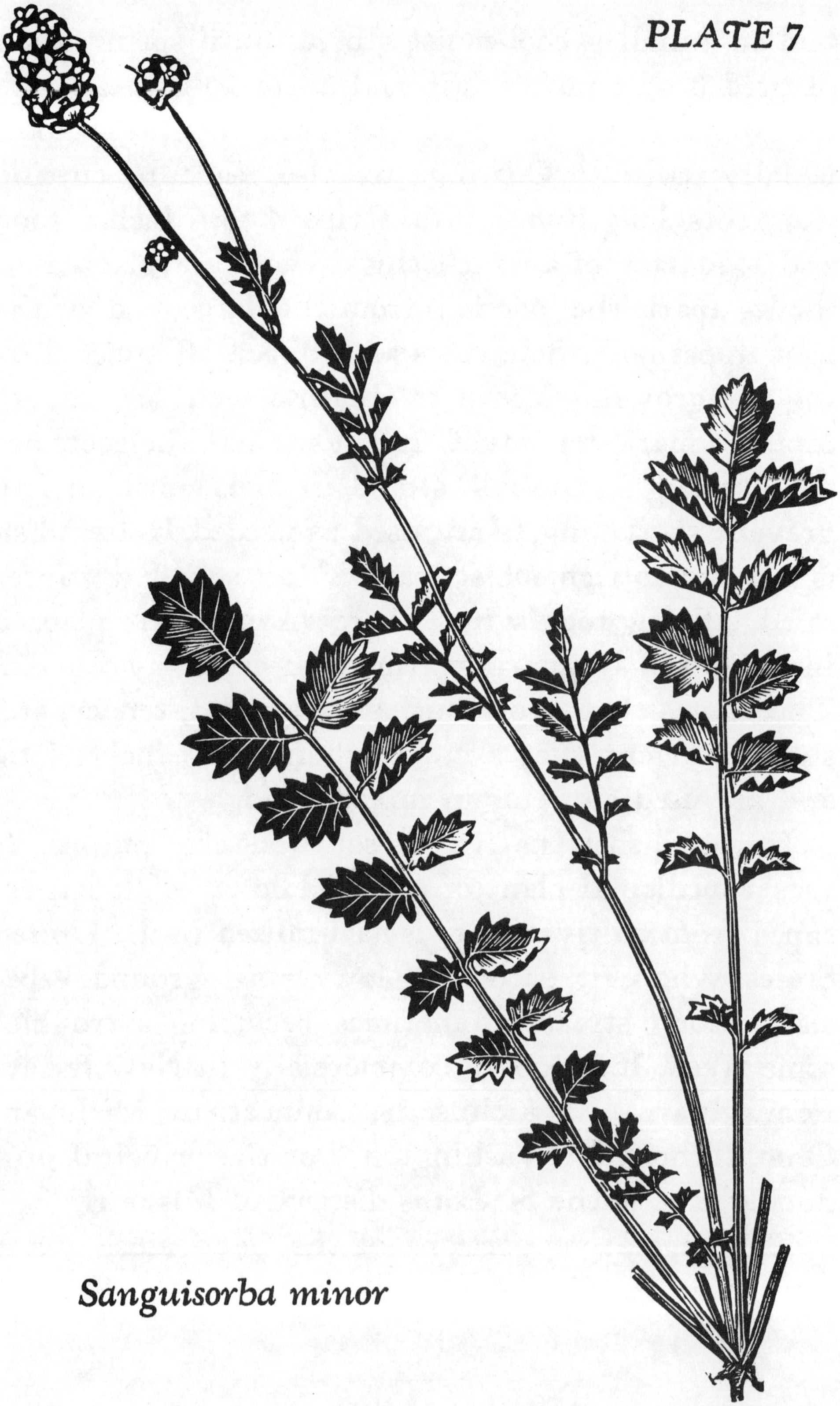

Sanguisorba minor

☾ ROSACEAE ⸱ ROSE FAMILY

DIVIDED INTO several tribes, this large family comprises about 2500 species in 100 genera. It is a diversified group of herbaceous & woody plants, held together by characters which they have more or less in common. Leaves are alternate & stipulate, the flowers regular, usually with numerous stamens, which are attached to the calyx; there are five petals. Such wild & cultivated fruits as the apple, cherry, pear, strawberry, blackberry, & raspberry belong to the family; also, besides the rose, such ornamentals as spiraea, hawthorn, shad bush, & geum.

SANGUISORBA MINOR Scop. ⸱ BURNET

Also called Pimpernel, Bloodwort, & Toper's Plant.
German: Bibernelle, Nagelkraut, Becherblume,
Kleiner Wiesenknopf. French: Pimprenelle.
Italian: Bibinella, Salvastrella.

A PERENNIAL plant, burnet produces numerous, alternate, dark-green, odd-pinnate leaves in a basal clump, the flowering stems reaching 20 inches. The leaflets are oblong to orbicular, their maximum length nearly 1 inch, margins notched or incised. The flowers are small, in globular, peduncled heads; they have no petals, but the calyx has petal-like lobes. The upper flowers are perfect, the lower staminate; the stamens are numerous & exserted, both stamens and stigmas purple. The fruit is a small, rough achene. Of value as an ornamental, burnet is also suitable for pasture or range grazing, being so used on calcareous soils in southern England. The leaves have a cucumber-like taste & odor when bruised. They are sometimes cooked as a pot-herb, & the fresh, young leaves are incorporated in salads, being too tough after blooming begins. They are used in preparing a tea beverage by infusion & for flavoring cold drinks and vinegar. Reputed to be useful in the treatment and healing of wounds, the roots are dried and ground and used as an astringent for internal bleeding. The dried & pounded seeds may be used to flavor vinegar. Burnet is a good subject for the garden border.

Propagation is by seeds, which germinate readily, and by root division. Burnet often self-sows, and is adapted to rather dry, moderately fertile, calcareous soil & full sun exposure. The production of leaves is stimulated by keeping the flower-stalks cut off.

Native in Europe & Asia, *Sanguisorba minor* has become naturalized on this continent from southeastern Canada to Maryland.

See Plate 7.

ℂ LEGUMINOSAE ⸱ PEA or PULSE FAMILY

A LARGE family of herbaceous plants, shrubs, and trees, the *Leguminosae* have members on nearly all large land masses throughout the world. Leaves are usually alternate & stipulate, mostly compound. Flowers are usually perfect, with ten stamens, five united sepals, and one pistil. The corolla is papilionaceous in most members of the family, which is divided into the pea tribe with papilionaceous flowers, the senna tribe with irregular but not papilionaceous flowers, & the mimosa tribe with regular flowers. The roots usually bear nodules or tubercles containing nitrogen-fixing bacteria.

TRIGONELLA FOENUM-GRAECUM L.
FENUGREEK

French: Fenugrec, Senegré. Italian: Fieno-greco.
German: Kuhhornklee, Griechisch-Heu.

AN ANNUAL, fenugreek is erect, usually not branching, pubescent, & reaches a height of 2 feet. Leaves are alternate, petioled, trifoliate, stipulate, the leaflets reaching a length of 1 inch. The flowers are white, axillary, solitary or two together, with short pedicels, & are papilionaceous. The fruit is a long, slender, beaked pod, which may reach 6 inches. The

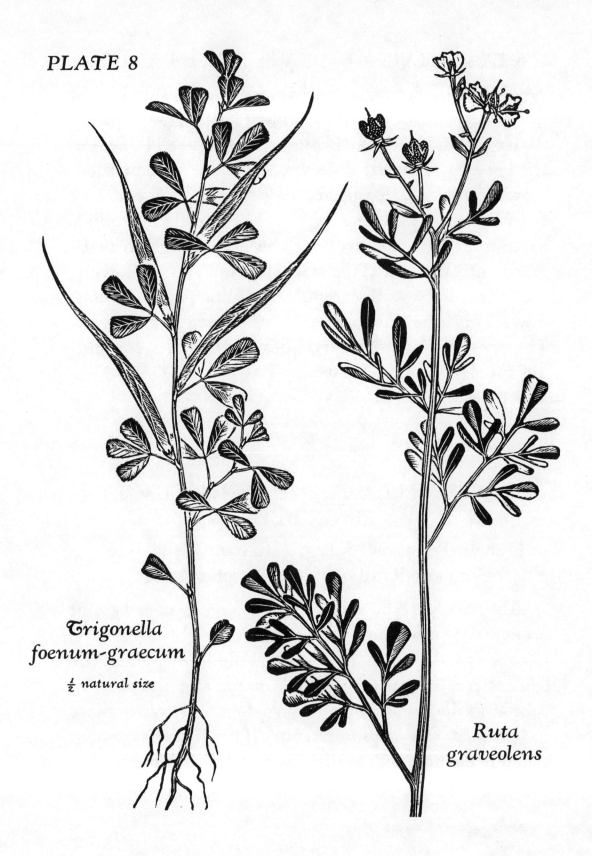

PLATE 8

Trigonella
foenum-graecum

½ natural size

Ruta
graveolens

seeds are small, brown, rhomboidal, & two-lobed.

In India the fresh plant is eaten as a vegetable; in Egypt the young seedlings are eaten raw. The plant is also grown for forage or mixed with other hay for livestock. The seeds are condimental & medicinal; they are used in curry powders & in plasters, ointments, & fever remedies; when soaked in water, the seeds swell & yield an emollient mucilage, which is used for treating digestive troubles. Ground seeds are incorporated in livestock condition powders. The extract together with other aromatics gives the flavor of maple & is used in confectionery.

The plants are propagated by seeds & respond to average garden culture, being best adapted to well-drained, medium loam. They are spaced 2 to 3 inches by 18 inches.

Native to southern Europe & Asia, especially the eastern shore of the Mediterranean Sea, fenugreek is cultivated in India & North Africa.

Plate 8 shows a plant in fruit.

PLATE 9

Dictamnus albus

⟪ RUTACEAE ⸱ RUE FAMILY

THIS IS the family of the citrus-fruits. The plants are mostly woody, the leaves either alternate or opposite, usually compound but sometimes with only one leaflet, often gland-dotted & more or less aromatic. The flowers have three to five sepals when present, & three to five petals; the stamens are from one to three times as many as the petals, arising from the base of a disk; the pistils are solitary or several. The fruit is of various types, dry or fleshy. There are about nine hundred species.

DICTAMNUS ALBUS L. ⸱ FRAXINELLA
Also called Gas Plant & Dittany.
French: Dictame blanc, Dictame commun, Fraxinelle.
German: Weisser Diptam, Weisse Aschwurz,
Spechtwurz, Springwurz.
Italian: Dittamobianco, Frasinella, Limonella.

A GARDEN ornamental & perennial, fraxinella produces numerous herbaceous shoots in a clump. attaining a height of 3 or more feet. Leaves are alternate, pinnately compound, gland-dotted, the margins serrulate. Flowers are numerous & showy, pinkish-purple or white, produced in terminal racemes. The fruits are five-lobed capsules which burst open with

41

force when thoroughly ripe & dry. The seeds are black & shiny. There are several horticultural varieties which differ in size of plant & color of flowers.

The leaves, preferably dried, are used in the preparation of a refreshing tea beverage, which is, however, not always liked by everyone. The root is said to be used as a remedy for hysteria & fevers. Gas plant is a curious & attractive garden ornamental.

The plant is difficult to propagate. Seeds should be planted as soon as ripe & may not germinate until the following year. Propagation is also by three-inch cuttings of the root, planted in spring. The plant is adapted to average garden conditions, responding best to rich soil. The roots are winter-hardy; the tops die to the ground in winter.

Contact with the seed-pods may cause a dermatitis in some susceptible persons, if the skin is exposed to sunlight after contact. Plate 9 shows seed-pods and leaves. Fraxinella is native in Europe & in Asia as far eastward as China.

RUTA GRAVEOLENS L. - RUE

German: Weinraute, Gartenraute, Kreuzraute.
French: Rue, Rue puante. Italian: Ruta.

RUE IS A perennial of herbaceous growth, but tends to be woody at the base. The plant is smooth, glaucous, bitter-aromatic, the stems erect, branched, reaching a height of about 3 feet. Leaves are alternate, pinnately divided two or three times, the segments obovate to cuneate, sometimes notched at the apex. The flowers have conspicuous yellow petals and grow in terminal clusters. The fruit is a dehiscent capsule with four or five lobes.

The plant is reputed to possess medicinal properties as a stimulant and as an aid for flatulence and colic. A bunch hung in a room is said to be repellent to flies & repellent to bedbugs if placed in a bed. The fresh leaves are sometimes pickled & are also used to flavor foods & beverages, being incorporated in salad, stews, ragouts, & sandwich-fillings; they also season vinegar & cocktails. The flavor, however, is due to an irritating essential oil, & the plant is probably not safe for human consumption. Some susceptible persons experience a dermatitis after contact with the leaves. Rue has ornamental value in the garden.

Propagation is by division, layers, cuttings, & seeds which germinate readily; rue self-sows. It is adapted to well-drained, calcareous soil containing some clay, and to full sun exposure. Spacing of the plants is from 18 to 24 inches.

Of ancient culture, rue was familiar to the Greeks and Romans, & to the medieval herbalists. Native in southern Europe, rue is now grown in many countries of the temperate zone. It is occasionally found wild as an escape in the northeastern United States.

Plate 8 shows the top of a plant in flower & fruit.

43

PLATE 10

*Anethum
graveolens*

ℂ UMBELLIFERAE • PARSLEY FAMILY

HERBACEOUS, hollow-stemmed plants make up most of this family. Besides the herbs described below, another useful member is the garden carrot, of which the wild form is a common weed. Two members, water-hemlock & water-parsnip, are poisonous. The leaves of the *Umbelliferae* are usually alternate & compound with enlarged or sheathing petiole bases. Flowers are small & borne in simple or compound umbels, secondary umbels being called umbellets. The fruit is a dry schizocarp, the two halves usually separating below & remaining attached to the central axis. Each half is one-seeded and often ridged, furrowed, & bristly; examples are shown in the illustrations of chervil & sweet cicely.

ANETHUM GRAVEOLENS L. • DILL

German: Dill, Dillfenchel, Gurkenkraut, Teufelsdill. French: Aneth, Fenouil puant. Italian: Aneto.

DILL IS A biennial, but is usually grown as an annual. The plant is stemmy & glaucous, with finely dissected, alternate leaves. It reaches a height of 2 or 3 feet & tends to fall down or lodge when mature. The yellow flowers are in large umbels.

The seeds & young leaves are condimental, the

latter used in beef gravy, cottage cheese, & potato salad, also for flavoring sauces, vinegars, soups, fish, cooked cabbage, cauliflower, & turnips. The seeds flavor sauces, gravies, apple pie, cakes, spiced beets, preserves, & vinegar. For dill pickles, the seed heads, with some stems & leaves, are cut when the seeds begin to ripen & are put in jars or crocks in alternate layers with cucumbers which are generously sprinkled with salt; the salt, drawing moisture from the cucumbers, creates a brine. Commercial pickles usually have vinegar added. Dill has medicinal properties, being carminative & stomachic.

Propagation is by seeds which germinate promptly, but the percentage of viable seed may be low. Dill often self-sows. The seed should be sown early, preferably indoors. Seventy-five days are required for the plants to mature. They should stand 8 to 12 inches apart in the row. Lodging of the plants may be prevented by the use of light stakes. Average garden soil is favorable for dill. The seed is harvested as soon as ripe by cutting the stems & spreading them out in a dry, shady, well-ventilated place. When thoroughly dry, the seed is threshed & cleaned.

Dill is a native of the Mediterranean region and was grown in ancient times. It occurs as a wild plant in the eastern United States from Connecticut to Virginia. It is also found wild in the West Indies.

Plate 10 shows the top of a blooming plant.

ANGELICA ARCHANGELICA L. - ANGELICA

French: Archangélique, Herbe du Saint-Esprit.
German: Angelica, Engelwurz, Giftwürze, Heiliger
Geist, Theriakwurzel. Italian: Angelica, Archangelica.

A BIENNIAL or short-lived perennial, angelica
may be made to live longer by keeping the plants
from flowering or fruiting. The third year commonly completes the plant's life, but offshoots are sometimes produced. The roots are long, spindle-shaped,
and fleshy. Stems are stout, hollow, fluted, glaucous,
reaching a height of about 7 feet. Leaves are alternate, glaucous, twice compound, the leaflets numerous, three-parted, the margins serrate; the bases are
dilated, clasping, reddish-purple. The inflorescence is
a large, compound umbel, with many small, whitish
flowers. Water-hemlock is sometimes confused with
angelica which it resembles. In angelica the secondary veins of the leaves end in the tips of the lobes,
rather than between them.

The leaflets are boiled & eaten like spinach but
are too bitter for general acceptance; the bitterness is
reduced by blanching & by boiling in two waters.
Parts of the herbage are added to the pot in which
fish is boiled & are also used as a garnish with fish
and meat dishes. Tender leafstalks & stems are used
for garnish, added to salad, & boiled or roasted like
potatoes. Blanched stems are eaten raw as a vegetable
like celery, & also in salads. The stems are cooked

PLATE 11

Angelica
archangelica

Two thirds natural size

with rhubarb & used to flavor rhubarb jam. Leaf-stalks & stems split lengthwise are candied by boiling in sugar syrup to which a little lemon may be added. Candied leafstalks constitute the commercial angelica, bought by confectioners for use in cakes, candy, & choice desserts; candied stems are used as decoration for pastry & candy when green coloring is wanted; they also help to flavor preserved fruits. The roots may also be candied. The stems and roots, eaten raw or cooked in various ways, are greatly esteemed as delicacies in the Scandinavian countries. The very aromatic, juniper-like flavor of angelica is too strong for most persons to enjoy raw; the odor, however, is very pleasing, & angelica water, formerly made from the leaves, was highly regarded as a perfume. Angelica seeds are used as a substitute for juniper berries for flavoring gin. They also flavor soft drinks, cakes, candies, comfits, & desserts; angelica is used in vanilla substitutes. The dried roots and fruits are ingredients of brandy, vermouth, Benedictine, & Chartreuse.

The medicinal value is principally in the fruits, although all parts of the plant are reputed to be carminative, antiflatulent, stimulant, diaphoretic, tonic, expectorant, & emollient for the stomach. An infusion of the dried leaves in boiling water is considered to be tonic, stimulant, & strengthening. An infusion of the chopped root in boiling water, combined with lemon, sugar, & whiskey, makes a good cough remedy. The plant is also considered to be a remedy for colds, chronic bronchitis, pleurisy, colic, rheumatism, kidney trouble, & indigestion. The popular names of the plant indicate its ancient reputation as a cure for almost every ailment.

Propagation is by seeds sown as soon as ripe in late summer or early autumn. Depth of planting is about one half inch. Seeds kept until the following spring should be stored under refrigeration; viability, however, decreases rapidly during storage. Fall-sown seeds should preferably be started in a seed-bed and the seedlings transplanted in spring to 30 inches a-part. The seeds may also be sown directly where the plants are to stand. Larger plants, even of moderate size, do not stand transplanting. Self-sown seedlings occasionally appear. Offshoots & divisions of old roots are occasionally used for propagation. Angelica is a-daptable in its soil requirements, but is favored by a fairly rich, light loam, which should be moist but well-drained. Partial shade and nearness to running water are beneficial but not essential. Roots are dug during the second autumn, cleaned, and then dried thoroughly by moderate heat. If kept in well-capped jars, they will retain their essential oil & volatile substances for a long time. Leaves are harvested in spring. The seeds should be harvested as soon as they are ripe & dried in warm air. Cutting off the tops of the plants before they are ready to flower lengthens the life of the roots indefinitely; they die off soon after flowers & fruits are produced.

Angelica is a plant of old-time gardens & herbal lore, its use dating from about 1500. It is native in Europe & Asia, especially in cool, northern climates, occurring wild in cool, moist places in Scotland, but more abundantly in Iceland, Lapland, & the areas along the southeastern shore of the Baltic Sea. The plant is grown commercially in England for candying the stems; candied leafstalks are a specialty of Clermont-Ferrand, Puy de Dome, France. Angelica root, one of the principal aromatics of European growth, is a special product of Germany & Spain.

Plate 11 shows flower-heads & a leaf.

ANTHRISCUS CEREFOLIUM Hoffm. - CHERVIL

Also called Beaked Parsley. French: Cerfeuil. German: Gartenkerbel, Kerbelkraut, Suppenkerbel, Körbel, Körfel. Italian: Cerfoglio, Mescolanza.

CHERVIL IS AN annual parsley-like plant with decompound, alternate leaves & small white flowers in compound umbels. The stem is four-sided & the plant somewhat hairy. The height sometimes reaches 2 feet, usually much less. There is a curl-leaved variety with the flavor & aroma of anise.

The leaves, resembling a mild parsley, are used for seasoning, for garnish, for salad, and as a pot-herb.

51

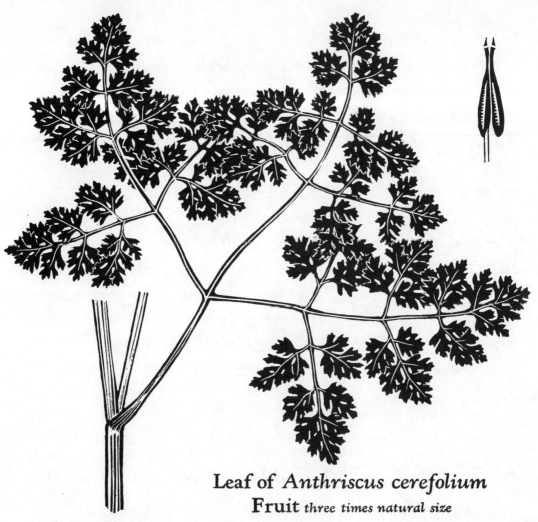

Leaf of *Anthriscus cerefolium*
Fruit *three times natural size*

Chopped leaves are incorporated in meat loaf, soups, egg dishes, fish sauces, salads, & salad dressing; they flavor vinegar & are used medicinally on bruises.

Propagation is by seeds which germinate promptly. The plants are favored by a medium, well-drained soil; they are subject to damage by wireworms, which attack the crowns & kill the plants.

Chervil is a native of southern Russia and the Caucasus region. In this country it has become naturalized as a wild plant in the northeastern states.

CARUM CARVI L. - CARAWAY

French: Carvi, Cumin, Anis de Vosges.
German: Wiesen-kümmel, Brot-kümmel.
Italian: Carvi, Cumino tedesco, Anice de Vosgi.

USUALLY grown as a biennial, caraway is herbaceous, with thick roots, a slender, erect stem, and decompound alternate leaves with narrow segments. The flowers are small & white, rarely pink, in compound umbels. The fruit is about one sixth of an inch long, brown, ridged & grooved. The height of the plant reaches 2 or 3 feet.

The roots are well-flavored & are boiled as a vegetable. The leaves & young shoots are cooked as a pot-herb & added to soups, also eaten raw in salads and added to cooked vegetable salad. The seeds are condimental & are used in rye bread, biscuits, rolls, cakes, cookies, cheese, baked apples, apple sauce, soups, and sauerkraut, & are sugar-coated for confectionery. The seeds are also medicinal; they are eaten for colic and indigestion & are munched after meals to prevent digestive disturbances; an infusion is made of one teaspoonful of chopped seeds to a cup of boiling water; the beverage is drunk slowly.

Caraway is propagated by seeds which should be harvested as soon as ripe; it sometimes self-sows. It is favored by a dry, clay soil.

The seeds (half-fruits or mericarps) are sometimes infested by the larvae of certain minute chalcid flies,

the pupation occurring within the seeds, the tiny, dark-colored adult flies emerging through small holes.

Native in Europe & western Asia, caraway occurs wild in North America from Newfoundland to Colorado. The leaves closely resemble carrot, but the umbels are looser, & their bracts are insignificant or lacking.

CHAEROPHYLLUM BULBOSUM L.
TURNIP-ROOTED CHERVIL

French: Carotte de Philadelphie, Cerfeuil bulbeux.
German: Kerbelrübe, Knollenkerbel, Rübenkerbel,
Peperlein, Pimperlipimp.

AN ERECT & branching biennial, turnip-rooted chervil reaches a height of 5 or 6 feet, growing from carrot-shaped roots or tubers, which are grayish on the outside & yellowish-white within. The stem is swollen below the nodes & is more or less hairy, especially below. The leaves are decompound, the ultimate segments narrow. The inflorescence is a many-rayed compound umbel. The mericarps are elongate, somewhat curved, & striped by dark furrows.

The roots are cooked like carrots or are added to stews; they are boiled or steamed and served with melted butter, salt, & pepper; they may also be fried like parsnips.

Propagation is by seeds, which germinate slowly and should be planted in the fall as soon as ripe or stratified in sand over winter. Roots are available for use in late summer or early fall, approximately five months after germination of the seeds. They may be stored over winter.

A native of central Europe & the Caucasus region, the plant is adaptable to garden culture but is not as well known here as it deserves to be.

The fruit & a typical leaf are shown in Plate 12.

PLATE 12

Three times
natural size

Chaerophyllum
bulbosum

CORIANDRUM SATIVUM L. - CORIANDER

French: Coriandre. German: Koriander, Wanzendill.
Italian: Coriandolo, Coriandro.

THE PLANT is annual, reaching a height of 2 or 3 feet. The leaves are alternate, twice or thrice decompound, the segments becoming successively narrower toward the top of the plant. The flowers are small, white or pinkish, in compound umbels, the petals of the outer flowers of each umbellet enlarged. The fruits are globular, ribbed, yellowish-brown and pleasantly aromatic when ripe; each fruit consists of two halves or mericarps. Intensely green, coriander is attractive in appearance, especially in full bloom, and is a good bee-plant; the foliage, however, has a disagreeable odor. Fruits shatter soon after maturity.

The seeds are sometimes candied as a confection. Ground or crushed seeds are used to flavor various beverages, breads, cakes, cookies, sweet rolls, cheese, bologna sausage, fish, meat sauce, ground meat, and spiced meat; they are incorporated in poultry dressing and pickles & are an ingredient of mixed spices of various kinds. They are sometimes used to improve the taste of medicines & are reputed to be stimulant, carminative, and stomachic. They are an ingredient of homemade clove liqueur, prepared according to the following directions:

In one pint of boiling water in a wide-mouthed vessel dissolve one quarter of a pound of sugar, allow

PLATE 13

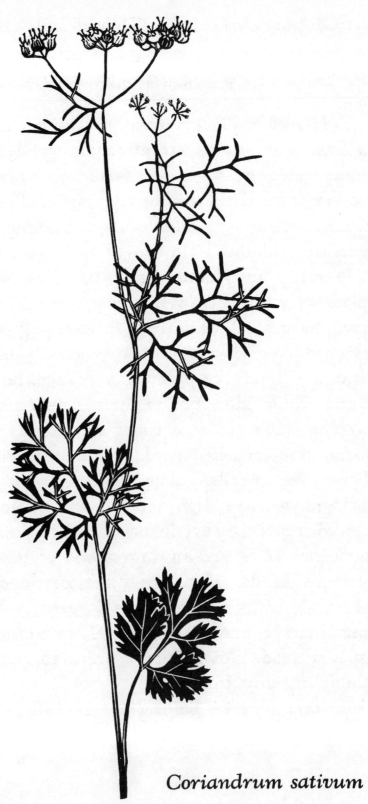

Coriandrum sativum

to cool, then add sufficient brandy to make one quart of liquid. Add one half ounce of ground cloves and one half ounce of ground coriander seeds, also twenty dried black cherries. Cork the mixture tightly and keep it in the sun or in a warm place for three or four weeks, shaking once a day. Then strain it into a dry, clean bottle & cork tightly.

Coriander is much esteemed in Peru. Mr. Victor Lionel Guzman of Lima, Peru, has given us this information regarding its use:

The leaves, used only in fresh condition, never dry, are picked early, well before the flowers start to develop. They are chiefly used to flavor two or three dishes, especially soup & a stew of the meat of young goat. Sometimes they are used to mask the odor of strong meats, the leaves being ground & mixed with the meat after cooking. A popular soup or stew in Peru, especially among the Indians, is prepared by first peeling, chopping, and boiling potatoes in a pot, to which is afterwards added a fried mixture of lard, onions, salt, & sometimes a little hot pepper for condiment. Eggs, cheese, & sometimes milk are put in at the end. After the pot has been removed from the fire, chopped fresh coriander leaves are sprinkled on top. The leaves may also be sprinkled on soups and stews after these are ladled into separate dishes for serving at the table.

Propagation of coriander is by seeds, which germinate quickly; they remain viable in storage for several years; they self-sow readily. The plant responds to average or medium garden soil & full sun. Spacing should be 8 to 10 inches apart. The seeds are harvested as soon as ripe.

Of ancient culture, coriander is mentioned in early Egyptian and Roman literature; it was used by the ancients to preserve meat. It is native in southern Europe & the Mediterranean region, where it is commonly grown; it is also cultivated in India, central Europe & England, & parts of Latin America, & is naturalized as a wild plant in waste areas throughout a large part of the United States.

Plate 13 shows the upper part of a plant in fruit.

CUMINUM CYMINUM L. - CUMIN

German: Kreuzkümmel, Aegiptischer Kümmel, Wanzenkümmel, Römischer Kümmel, Pfefferkümmel. French: Cumin. Italian: Comino, Cimino.

A SMALL glabrous annual, with a thin, branched, angular stem, cumin reaches a height of 6 to 12 inches, and has alternate, dark green, dissected leaves with filiform segments, the tips of which are often recurved. The flowers are white or pinkish, in compound umbels. The fruits are oblong & bristly; they are the parts for which cumin is grown, the vegetative parts not being of practical use. The seeds are

PLATE 14

*Cuminum
cyminum*

aromatic & condimental, but of an unpleasant flavor.

They are used in flavoring pastry, cheeses, soups, pickles, alcoholic liquors, & sauerkraut, and form an ingredient of curry powder. Although having medicinal properties like caraway, cumin seed, because of its peculiar flavor, is used only in veterinary medicine. Cumin is stimulant, carminative, antiflatulent, and is also used in the composition of a liniment.

Propagation is by seeds which germinate readily and remain viable in storage for several years. Cumin is adapted to average garden conditions & matures in about sixty days.

Known to the ancients and used as a spice and a medicine during the Middle Ages, the plant is native in the Mediterranean region. It has long been cultivated in China & North Africa, as well as in India, where it is still employed in human medicine.

See Plate 14.

FOENICULUM VULGARE Mill. - FENNEL

French: Fenouil. German: Fenchel. Italian: Finocchio.

ALTHOUGH perennial, fennel is usually grown as an annual or as a biennial. The plant is erect, the stems smooth & glossy, reaching a height of 4 or 5 feet. The leaves are finely divided into filiform segments & have enlarged, sheathing bases. The yellow

PLATE 15

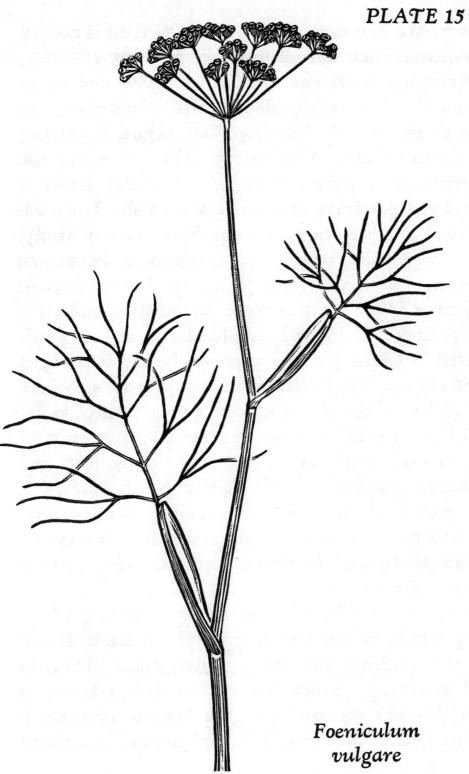

*Foeniculum
vulgare*

flowers are in compound umbels. The fruit is oblong, one quarter inch long, smooth, & strongly ribbed.

Anise-like in flavor, the tender leaves and stems are used as a pot-herb, salad, or relish; leaves are also used as garnish or flavoring. Cut before flowering, the stems are eaten like celery. The leaves are also incorporated in soups, stews, & fish sauces; fennel is considered particularly suitable with fish. The seeds are used for flavoring puddings, breads, cakes, candy, soups, vegetables, sauerkraut, & alcoholic beverages; they are also used to modify the taste of unpleasant medicines & are reputed to be carminative, sudorific, and pectoral. The root is edible, the plant being cultivated in China for this purpose. Fennel is thought to be effective in flea-repellent preparations. When in full bloom, the plants attract a great many wasps.

A liqueur similar to the one mentioned on page 57 may be made with fennel seeds. The ingredients and measurements are: one & a half cups of water, one half pound of sugar, four & a half cups of brandy, one half ounce of fennel seeds, one half inch piece of cinnamon stick, & six cloves. Anise seed may be substituted for fennel.

Propagation is by seeds, which germinate quickly. They should be sown where the plants are to stand, and the seedlings thinned to 1 foot apart. They do well in average garden soil but are best adapted to light, dry soil containing a good amount of lime.

One form of the common fennel has bronze-colored

leaves & is known as "copper" or "bronze" fennel. Another is variety *piperitum*, known as Italian or Sicilian fennel or carosella, which is cultivated for its edible stems. Of ancient culture, fennel is native in southern Europe & the Mediterranean region; it occurs as an escape in the United States from southern New England to Louisiana, being most frequent in Maryland & Virginia.

Plate 15 shows the top of a plant.

FOENICULUM VULGARE Mill. var. DULCE Fiori
FLORENCE FENNEL, FINOCCHIO

THIS IS A modified form of common fennel, the leaf bases greatly enlarged & the plant shorter and more compact. The base of the plant, with its thick, overlapping leaf bases, resembles celery.

Usually blanched, the leaf bases may be eaten raw with salad dressing, or boiled. The green tops may be cooked as a pot-herb or used raw as a garnish.

The seed should be sown in rows 16 to 20 inches apart, & the seedlings thinned to 6 inches apart. The plants need a great deal of water. When the bases are about an inch thick, they should be hilled up to blanch them. They are ready for use in about ten days; another sowing may be made three weeks after the first one.

65

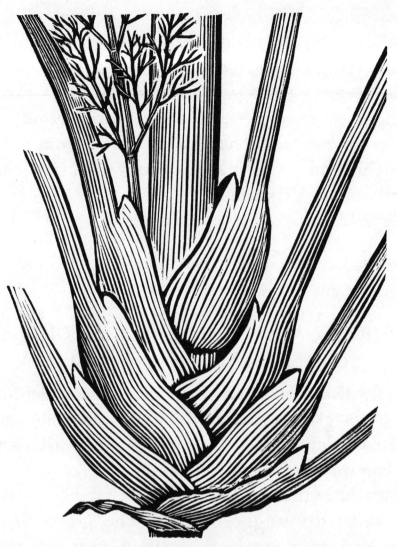

Basal portion of FLORENCE FENNEL

Finocchio is a common vegetable in Italy & is also grown and eaten by the Italian population of the United States. The flavor is too sweet for average American taste.

It is thought that this variety may have originated in the Azores.

LEVISTICUM OFFICINALE Koch - LOVAGE
Also called Smellage & Smallage.
French: Livèche, Ache des montagnes, Céléri bâtard.
German: Berg-Liebstöckel.
Italian: Levistico, Ligustico, Sedano montano.

A TALL, vigorous, perennial plant, lovage may reach a height of 7 feet. It has alternate, ternately decompound leaves, the ultimate segments broad, flat, and wedge-shaped. The flowers are greenish-yellow or whitish-yellow, in umbels. The fruits are very aromatic, small, elliptical, curved, yellowish-brown, each mericarp with three winged ribs. The herbage has a celery-like flavor & an agreeable aroma, which, however, is sometimes weak or lacking. The stout, fluted stem rises from a thick rhizome or rootstock, which has a pronounced taste & fragrance.

The leaves, fresh or dried, are suitable for flavoring salads, sauces, soups, & stews as a substitute for celery, and are used to make a tea beverage. They should be gathered when young and tender, at the time of new, flush growth, the stage shown in Plate 16. They may be boiled for a pot-herb or rubbed on the inside of the salad bowl to impart a flavor; the dried leaves are good in herb blends. Petioles & stem-bases are sometimes blanched & eaten raw like celery or may be candied. The rootstock is similarly used, and the fruits are used to flavor candies & cordials.

Both roots & fruits are reputed to be diaphoretic

PLATE 16

Two thirds
natural size

*Levisticum
officinale*

and carminative and have been used as remedies for indigestion, fevers, colic, & flatulence. The plant has ornamental value in the garden. Escaped plants are relished by grazing cattle.

Propagation is by root division in spring, and by seeds, which are sown as soon as ripe in late summer. When the seedlings appear they should be thinned to stand 12 inches apart. Lovage is adapted to moist, fertile soil and either full sun or partial shade. Authentic viable seed is difficult to obtain; seeds of wild and cultivated celery (*Apium graveolens* & *A. graveolens* variety *dulce*) are often sold as lovage. Wild celery, also called smallage, is a low, white-flowered plant; the relative appearance of celery and lovage leaves is shown in the illustration below.

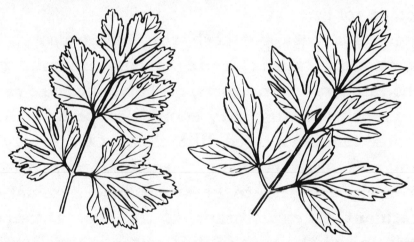

Lovage is a native of southern Europe, where it grows wild in the mountainous districts. It occurs wild as an escape along roadsides in the northeastern United States.

MYRRHIS ODORATA Scop. - SWEET CICELY

Also called Myrrh & Sweet Chervil.
French: Cerfeuil musqué, Cerfeuil anisé, Myrrhide.
German: Anis-Kerbel, Wohlriechende Süssdolde,
Wilder Anis, Welscher Kerbel, Ewiger Kerbel.
Italian: Finocchiella, Mirride.

A STOUT-ROOTED perennial, sweet cicely may reach a height of 3 feet. The stems are branching, the leaves alternate, pinnately decompound, fern-like, the ultimate segments lanceolate & toothed. Flowers are small & white, in compound umbels. The fruits are large, sometimes an inch long, ribbed, & dark brown, almost black. The whole plant is somewhat hairy, aromatic, anise-flavored; it is ornamental and attractive to bees.

Often used as a pot-herb, the leaves also flavor soups, stews, & salads. Young shoots are mild and may be eaten raw. The roots, raw or boiled, are eaten with French dressing; they should be peeled. Dried seeds are sometimes used like cloves & caraway in cooking and food flavoring. Medicinal properties of sweet cicely are said to be stomachic, carminative, antiflatulent, & expectorant, & the root antiseptic. An infusion of the root in hot water is considered a cough remedy.

Propagation is by root division in fall or spring, and by seeds planted in the fall as soon as ripe; they will not germinate until spring. The plant is adapted

70

to average garden soil & is favored by partial shade.

Sweet cicely is native in Europe where it grows wild in the higher elevations. It was known to the ancients & to the medieval herbalists. A plant of old-time gardens, it has had an undeserved decline in popularity.

A leaf & a fruit at natural size are shown above.

71

PLATE 17

Petroselinum crispum

Pimpinella anisum

One half
natural size

PETROSELINUM CRISPUM Nym. - PARSLEY

French: Persil. German: Petersilie, Peterchen.
Italian: Petroselino, Petrosello, Persemolo, Erborina.

A BIENNIAL or a perennial of short duration, parsley is a very leafy, dark green, smooth, aromatic plant, which produces a rosette of radical leaves the first growing season & a flowering stalk the second. The leaves are alternate, twice-pinnate or ternately decompound, the ultimate segments ovate, cuneate-ovate, or sometimes linear-oblong; the margins are incised, dentate, or entire; the segments may be partially reflexed. The flower-stalk is 18 inches to 3 feet high & bears small, greenish-yellow flowers in peduncled compound umbels. The fruits are smooth, ribbed, ovate, about one tenth inch long, the half-fruits or mericarps at maturity bent slightly outward, except at top & bottom. Main horticultural varieties of parsley include plain or flat-leaved, fern-leaved, curled or moss-leaved, Hamburg or parsnip-rooted, cultivated for its fleshy root, which is used like celery root to flavor soups & stews, & Neapolitan or celery-leaved, grown for its esculent stems.

Best known & most commonly grown of all the herbs, parsley is used as a garnish with meat, fish, egg, cheese, vegetable, & salad dishes. It is eaten out of hand, incorporated in salad, chopped & sprinkled on cooked vegetables, used as an ingredient of soups, stews, sauces, & omelettes; it is sometimes used as a

73

pot-herb & to make a tea, which is antiscorbutic; dried leaves are not efficacious for this purpose, but are much used for flavoring. Mild medicinal properties have been attributed to the seeds & roots. Parsley has the useful property of masking strong odors. The leaf rosettes of the curly variety make a neat and ornamental edging for flower beds.

Propagation is by seeds, which are commonly considered slow in germinating; in our investigation the seed germinated with satisfactory promptness. Germination is stimulated by soaking in water before planting. Seeds are harvested the second spring and remain viable about three years, germinating better after a period of storage than when fresh. The plants may be started indoors & later set out, or they may be started outdoors in spring as soon as the ground can be worked. Planting may be done in midsummer for a fall crop. The rows should be 18 inches apart and the plants 6 to 8 apart in the row, except the parsnip-rooted variety, which may be spaced 4 inches apart. Parsley is adapted to average fertile garden soil and is favored by abundant moisture & some shade. New leaves grow as the older ones are cut off. Plants may be grown indoors in flower pots & window boxes & will remain green all winter if protected from freezing.

Parsley is native in the Mediterranean region. On this continent it occurs wild from Ontario to Maryland. Plate 17 shows a leaf & an inflorescence.

PIMPINELLA ANISUM L.-ANISE

Also called Sweet Cumin, Sweet Alice, Heal-bite.
French: Anis. German: Anis. Italian: Anice, Anacio.

THE PLANT is annual, usually erect, sometimes
sprawling, & reaches a height of 2 feet or more. The
basal & stem leaves differ, the basal ones being long-
stalked & either simple or thrice compound, & the
margins coarsely toothed; the stem leaves are alternate, once or twice pinnate or ternately compound,
the leaflets, lobes, or segments becoming narrower and
finer toward the top of the plant. The flowers are
small & yellowish-white in large, compound, terminal umbels. The fruits are gray or greenish, ribbed
and furrowed, slightly downy, aromatic & sweet-
flavored, about one eighth inch long. See Plate 17.

Fresh leaves are used as a garnish, for flavoring
salads, & for cooking as a pot-herb. The seeds are
the important part of the plant & are used to flavor
bread, rolls, cookies, cake, candy, soups, stews, cheese,
baked apples, & apple sauce; ground seeds are incorporated in sachet & curry powders & are used for a
tea drink, which is reputed to be stimulant, carminative, & a remedy for catarrh & bronchial troubles.

Propagation is by seeds, which should be sown
where the plants are to grow, to avoid transplanting.
Seeds harvested the preceding year are preferable.
Anise is adapted to rich, well-drained soil & full sun.

It is native in the eastern Mediterranean region.

75

PLATE 18

Borago officinalis

❡ BORAGINACEAE · BORAGE FAMILY

FOR THE most part, the *Boraginaceae* consist of herbaceous, bristly plants with white, pink, or blue flowers in cymes which are at first coiled, but straighten as the flowers open. The leaves are simple, the flowers symmetrical, with five-parted calyx and corolla & five stamens. There are about 1500 members in the family; three familiar ones are heliotrope, comfrey, & the forget-me-nots which belong to the genera *Cynoglossum, Anchusa,* & *Myosotis.*

BORAGO OFFICINALIS L. - BORAGE

German: Borretsch, Gurkenkraut.
French: Bourrache. Italian: Boragine.

A RANK, spreading annual, borage has succulent stems, reaching a height of 2 feet or more, & rough, hairy, alternate leaves, the older ones reaching 6 inches in length. The bright blue flowers are numerous, clustered, drooping, star-shaped, with striking black anthers. Plate 18 shows a young plant and a single flower. An excellent bee-plant, borage blooms all season & is very ornamental. The fresh herbage has a cucumber-like flavor & aroma.

The tender, young, upper leaves & sometimes the flowers are used in salads, pickles, cakes, iced drinks, and as a salad garnish; the leaves, thought to have a cooling effect in beverages, are put into claret-cup and other punches. Claret-cup consists of iced claret, a little brandy, sugar, & sliced lemon; mint may be substituted for borage. The young herbage is also cooked as a pot-herb, & the flowers are candied to make an old-fashioned sweetmeat. The plant contains abundant mucilage, potassium nitrate, & other salts. Its medicinal properties are mild; an infusion of the leaves & flowers is used as a demulcent, emollient, refrigerant, weak diaphoretic, diuretic, & aperient; it is employed in the treatment of catarrh, rheumatism, & skin diseases. The dried flowers are used in potpourri. The hairy leaves may cause a dermatitis when handled by susceptible individuals.

Propagation is by seeds sown in spring; germination is rapid; borage often self-sows. Seeds have been reported to remain viable for several years. Borage is cosmopolitan in its soil adaptation, but it responds to good soil conditions. Spacing of the plants should be 18 inches to 2 feet. Hot weather favors the growth of borage. Harvesting the seeds needed for propagation is a difficult process because of uneven ripening and early shattering; they may be collected on sheets of cloth or paper laid on the ground under the plants and weighted down.

Borage is native in the Mediterranean region, including southern Europe & North Africa. It occurs wild in the northeastern United States.

ℂ VERBENACEAE ⋅ VERVAIN FAMILY

A FAMILY represented mainly in tropical regions, the *Verbenaceae* consist of shrubs, herbaceous plants, & trees, of which teak is an example. The leaves are mostly opposite, sometimes whorled, and rarely alternate. The flowers are perfect, usually irregular, & the inflorescence is of various types. The petals are united, forming a tubular, four- or five-lobed corolla. There are either two stamens or four, arranged in two pairs of unequal length. The ovary is entire.

LIPPIA CITRIODORA HBK ⋅ LEMON VERBENA

French: Vervaine citronnelle. German: Zitron-verbene.

A TENDER perennial shrub adapted to mild climates, lemon verbena should be kept indoors during the winter in the North. It is normally deciduous and sometimes reaches a height of 15 feet, usually much less. The lemon-scented leaves are narrow and pointed, short-stalked, entire or slightly toothed, 2 to 4 inches long, in whorls of three or four, & gland-dotted on the under side. The flowers are in axillary spikes or terminal panicles; they are small, white or lilac-white, & have a four-lobed corolla & four stamens. Plate 19 shows an inflorescence & a flower.

The leaves are used to flavor beverages, desserts,

PLATE 19

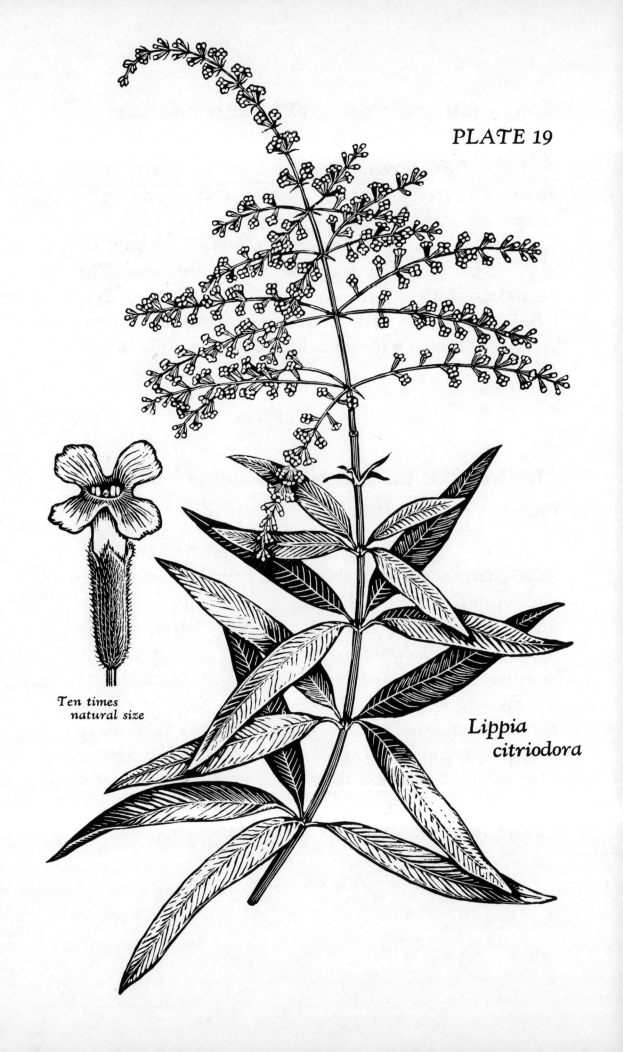

Ten times
natural size

*Lippia
citriodora*

fruit salads, melons, & jellies, and may be used for making a tisane. A decoction of the leaves & flowers is reputed to be febrifugal, sedative, stomachic, antispasmodic, & antiflatulent. The leaves are added to finger bowls & are used in cologne & sachets.

Propagation is by seeds & by cuttings of immature wood rooted under glass. Grown indoors in pots in winter, the plants may be bedded outdoors in summer. They are favored by light soil & full sun.

Native in Argentina, Chile, & Peru, lemon verbena is now naturalized in southern Europe & is a garden plant in many countries.

⟪ LABIATAE ⟋ MINT FAMILY

THE MINT family is a group of herbaceous and shrubby plants, usually with four-sided stems, and often aromatic, odorous, or bitter. The leaves are simple, opposite or whorled. Flowers are commonly irregular, calyx & corolla each composed of united parts, the calyx usually five-lobed and the corolla two-lipped, the lower lip being three-lobed. There are two or four stamens, & the ovary is four-lobed. The family is well-represented in all the temperate regions of the world.

81

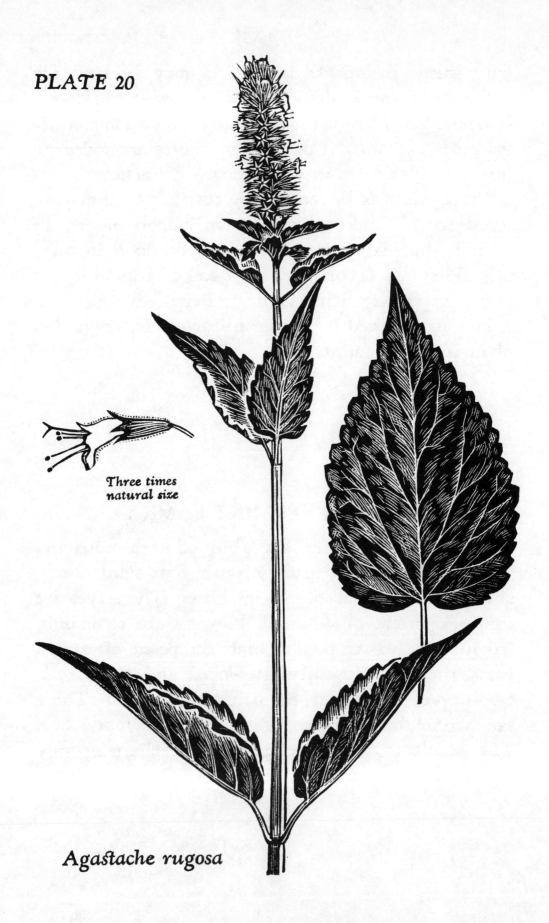

PLATE 20

Three times
natural size

Agastache rugosa

AGASTACHE FOENICULUM Kuntze
ANISE HYSSOP or GIANT FENNEL HYSSOP

A TALL perennial, anise hyssop reaches a height of 3 or 4 feet. It is smooth, except for the underside of the leaves, which are downy-white. The leaves are ovate to deltoid-ovate, acute, petioled, margins coarsely toothed, & bases usually rounded; the length may reach 3 to 4 inches. The blue flowers are in large terminal spikes. There are two pairs of stamens, the upper pair pointing downward, the lower curved upward, so that the pairs cross one another.

Anise hyssop is a wild plant, native on this continent & found chiefly in the north central area of the United States. It was much used by the American Indians & is now cultivated for its strongly anise-scented foliage. An aromatic tea is made from the leaves, which are also used dried or fresh for flavoring, much as sage is used. It is an excellent bee-plant.

Propagation is by seeds, which germinate readily. The plants are adaptable in their soil requirements, but need full sun & should be spaced 2 feet apart.

AGASTACHE RUGOSA Kuntze - KOREAN MINT

THIS SPECIES reaches a height of about 4 feet. The leaves are petioled, ovate, usually heart-shaped at the base, pointed at the tip, both surfaces hairy, margins coarsely toothed. The flowers are violet or rose-violet, in large spikes; the arrangement of the stamens is like that of the preceding species and is characteristic of *Agastache*. Plate 20 shows the top of a flowering stem & a single flower enlarged. Anise hyssop & Korean mint are similar in general aspect. Both have the flavor of anise.

Korean mint is used like anise hyssop & is likewise a good bee-plant. It does well in average garden conditions. It requires full sun. The plants should be spaced about 30 inches apart.

Agastache rugosa is a native of Japan & eastern China. In 1947, while serving as horticulturist for the United States Army Military Government in Korea, Professor E. M. Meader of the University of New Hampshire collected seeds of this plant, which he called Korean mint, & brought them to this country. Two collections were made, one from the king's Zoo Palace grounds in Seoul, & one from the Pouk Han Mountains. As far as is known, this is the first introduction of the plant into the United States.

HYSSOPUS OFFICINALIS L. - HYSSOP

French: Hyssope, Herbe sacrée.
German: Ysop. Italian: Issopo.

A PERENNIAL, woody at the base, hyssop has herbaceous stems which reach a height of 2 feet. The leaves are opposite, narrow, pointed, sessile, 1 to 2 inches long. The small blue flowers are in whorls, which are grouped on terminal spikes. The plant is aromatic & bitter-flavored. There are several horti-cultural varieties of hyssop characterized by flower and leaf variations; some have pink or white flowers.

Hyssop's strong flavor discourages its use for cooking, but the fresh shoot-tips, including leaves, stems, and flowers, have been used in flavoring cooked vegetables, soups, & even salads; dried leaves are used in herb blends for flavoring. Leaves & tops are steeped for a tea, which is said to be valuable for relieving coughs, colds, & dyspepsia, & to be aperient, laxative, and mildly stimulating. Ornamental in the garden, hyssop is also a good bee-plant. The essential oil is an ingredient of liqueurs & perfumes. If material for out-of-season use is required, the tender upper stems, flowering shoots, and flowers should be cut, dried, stripped, & pulverized & kept in tight jars. Flowers may be mixed with the leaves.

Propagation is by root division, cuttings, & seeds, the last being most used, since germination is good. Seeds remain viable several years. A light, alkaline soil with good drainage is favorable. The plants do well in sun or partial shade & may be spaced about a foot apart in the rows.

Hyssop is native in Europe & the temperate zone of Asia; it is probably not the hyssop of the Bible. It is naturalized here on the Pacific Coast & from southeastern Canada to North Carolina.

See Plate 21.

85

PLATE 21

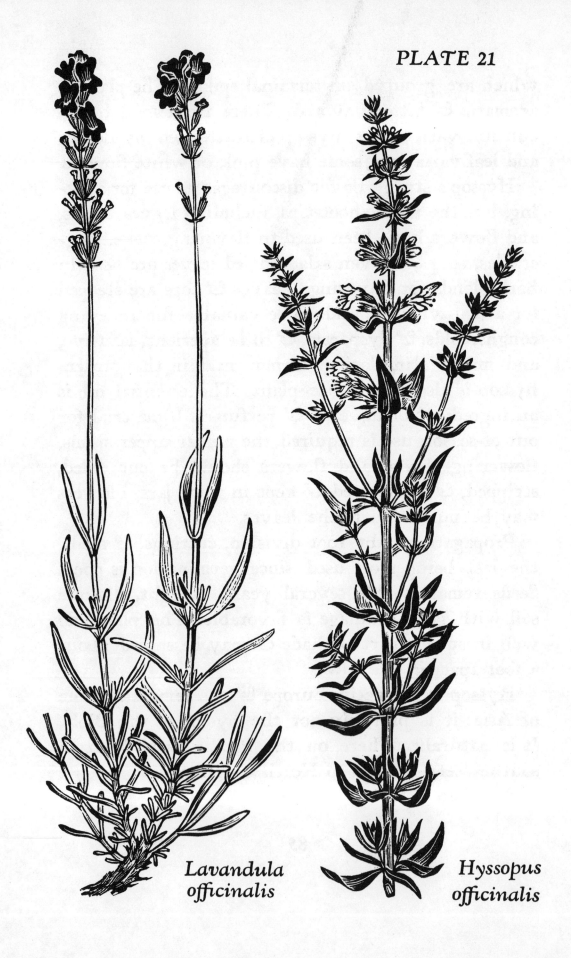

Lavandula officinalis

Hyssopus officinalis

LAVANDULA OFFICINALIS Chaix.
ENGLISH LAVENDER or TRUE LAVENDER

French: Lavande. German: Lavendel. Italian: Lavanda.

A SEMISHRUB reaching 3 feet, lavender is partially woody at the base, but the young stems are herbaceous. They are covered with a gray, velvety pubescence, as are the leaves. Narrow, linear, & opposite, the leaves are mostly revolute-margined, and may reach 2 inches in length. The small blue flowers are in whorls subtended by short, pointed bracts, the whorls in spikes on slender, wiry stems. There are many horticultural varieties of *Lavandula officinalis*, dwarf forms & color forms, ranging through white, rose, & many shades of purple & lavender. *L. spica* and *L. vera* are older names for *L. officinalis* & are no longer in use. A plant is shown in Plate 21.

The leaves & flower buds are occasionally used in flavoring foods, especially salads, dressings, fruit desserts, jelly, & wine; the flowers may be candied; a decoction of them is said to be stimulant and tonic; dried, they are used in sachet bags & placed among stored linens. The dried leaves are also so used; the odor is said to be insect-repellent. Lavender oil is of great importance in the manufacture of perfume, especially in England, where most of the finest oil is produced; great care is required in raising the plants, harvesting the flowers just at the height of bloom, and distilling them immediately after cutting. Plants

87

must be replaced every few years. Weather conditions at harvesting time have an important effect on the quality of the oil, ideal days for cutting being dry, still, & preceded by weeks of sunshine. Lavender oil is also used to some extent in medicine. Plants are ornamental, adapted to rock garden culture, and are an excellent source of honey.

Propagation is by root division in spring, by seeds, and by cuttings. Seeds remain viable about five years but are slow to germinate; one disadvantage of using seeds is that only certain strains of lavender are winter-hardy, and seed obtained from untested sources may not produce plants that will survive any but mild winters. Cuttings root readily & are the usual means employed. Lavender is adapted to light, dry, calcareous soil & full sun. The plants tend to spread, large ones requiring up to 30 inches of space.

All lavenders are native in the Mediterranean region. Three other commonly cultivated species are briefly mentioned below.

L. stoechas, called in German Schopflavendel or Welscher lavendel, in Italian Steca or Stigadosso, is a narrow-leaved species, the leaves half an inch long; the small flowers & prominent terminal bracts are purple. The plant is shrubby & is an inhabitant of coastal regions, being especially frequent in Spain. It is sometimes called French lavender.

L. latifolia closely resembles *L. officinalis*, but has wide, flat leaves. It grows in the higher elevations of southern France & Spain. In France, where an inferior oil is distilled from it, it is called Grande lavande or Aspic. In German it is Grosser Speik, & in Italian Spigo Nardo or Golgemma. English names are broad-leaved or spike lavender.

L. dentata, called fringed green or French lavender, has long, velvety, gray or green leaves, which are pinnately dentate, the teeth broad and nearly square at the tips.

❧

MAJORANA HORTENSIS Moench.
SWEET or KNOTTED MARJORAM

French: Marjolaine. Italian: Maggiorana, Amaraco. German: Majoran, Mairan, Wurstkraut.

A TENDER perennial, sweet marjoram is grown as an annual in northern gardens. The plant is erect, branched, & grows to a height of 2 feet. The downy, light green leaves are opposite, elliptical, entire, and petioled; the blades reach an inch in length. The minute white flowers are in whorls arranged in short, clustered spikes; the round, overlapping bracts give the spikes a knotted appearance. The flowers sometimes have a pink or lilac tint.

The leaves and flowering tops are used fresh or dried to flavor cooked vegetables, salads, stuffings, dressings, sausage, stews, soups, and sauces, also egg, meat, & fish dishes. Fresh leaves are used as garnish, incorporated in salads, & used to flavor vinegar. The herbage is reputed to be tonic, stimulant, & helpful to digestion; the infusion is employed as a remedy for headache & asthma. The dried flowering tops are suitable for sachets & potpourri. Sweet marjoram is often grown as a house plant.

Propagation is by seeds & occasionally by cuttings from plants kept indoors over winter. The seeds are very small & may be mixed with sand before scattering; although slow to germinate, they should not be sown until the ground has become warm.

Sweet marjoram is native in the Mediterranean region. Plate 22 shows the top of a plant at an early stage of bloom.

Majorana onites, called pot marjoram, is but little known in this country; plants sold under that name are usually M. *hortensis*, which it closely resembles, except that pot marjoram has sessile leaves, more numerous floral spikes, & is not so branched; its flavor is milder. It will be noted that one of the common names for *Origanum vulgare* is also pot marjoram.

Origanum majorana & O. *onites* are names no longer used for M. *hortensis* & M. *onites*.

ORIGANUM VULGARE L.-WILD MARJORAM

Also called Pot Marjoram, Winter Sweet,
Organy, and Oregano.*
French: Marjolaine sauvage, Origan.
German: Wilder Majoram, Gemeiner Dosten.
Italian: Maggiorana selvatica, Regamo.

A HARDY perennial, growing from a horizontal rhizome, wild marjoram has erect, branching stems that reach a height of 3 feet & form clumps. The stems are hairy, four-angled, often purplish. Leaves are petioled, entire or nearly so, round-ovate, rather dark green, & coarsely hairy. Flowers are purplish, pink, or lilac, sometimes almost white; the calyx is hairy. The flowers are in corymbose clusters of more or less cylindrical spikes with large, imbricated, purplish bracts. Besides the color forms mentioned above, there are other varieties of *Origanum vulgare*, differing in color of stem & leaf, form of spike, & so on; one has variegated leaves.

The plant has an aromatic, thyme-like flavor. The leaves & tops cut prior to blooming are used to flavor foods in the same way as sweet marjoram. They are sometimes cooked as a pot-herb & are used to make a tea said to be stimulant. The plant was formerly used to flavor ale & beer, before hops were introduced into the brewing industry.

Propagation is by root division, cuttings, layers, and seeds sown in spring; it self-sows freely and is

*Also spelled more correctly *origano*.

PLATE 22

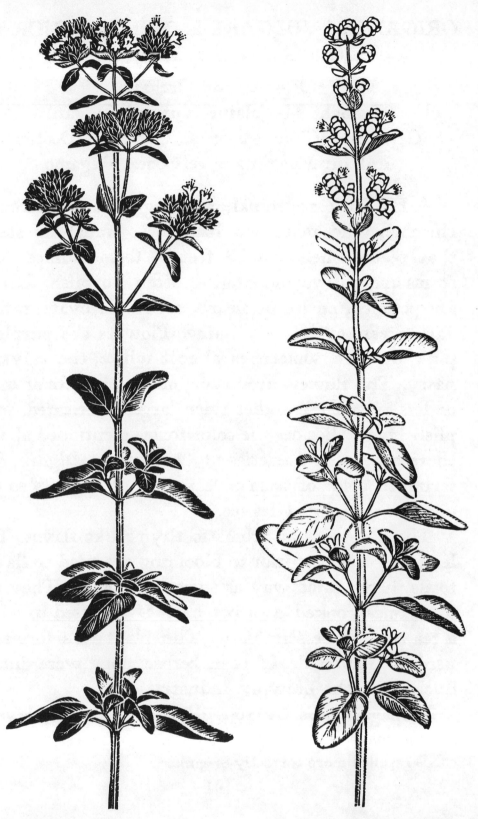

Origanum vulgare   *Majorana hortensis*

adapted to average garden soil & full sun exposure.

Native in Eurasia, wild marjoram is naturalized in the northeastern United States & Ontario; it is a weed in some localities. It is found in pastures, old fields, and waste places, in dry soil. See Plate 22.

❦

AMARACUS DICTAMNUS Benth.
DITTANY OF CRETE or HOP MARJORAM

French: Dictame. German: Kretische Diptam.
Italian: Dittamo cretico.

A TENDER perennial, dittany of Crete is a wiry, branched, more or less erect plant, not more than a foot high; it tends to be woody at the base. It has short-petioled, thick, orbicular leaves invested with a woolly pubescence. The overlapping floral bracts form hop-like spikes; the flowers are purplish-pink. Plate 23 shows a plant beginning to flower.

The plant is used to flavor salads; it is an ingredient of vermouth and is reputed to be useful for treating scrofula; the flowers are a tea substitute.

Propagation is by seeds & by cuttings, which root readily. Plants are grown indoors in pots in winter and bedded outside in the garden in summer. They are favored by dry, sandy soil and full sun. Spacing should be about 6 inches apart.

The plant is indigenous on the island of Crete.

PLATE 23

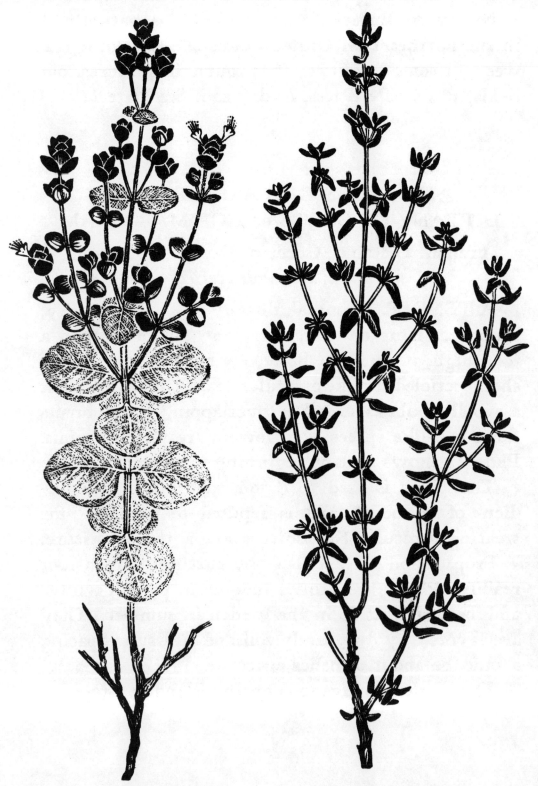

Amaracus dictamnus   *Thymus vulgaris*

THYMUS VULGARIS L. - GARDEN THYME

French: Thym, Farigoule. German: Thymian.
Italian: Timo, Erbuccia, Pepolino.

AN ERECT, clump-forming perennial, thyme is woody toward the base, the stems wiry & much branched; the plant reaches a height of 12 inches. The gray-green leaves are ovate to linear-ovate, one quarter to one half inch long, entire, sessile, the margins revolute. The minute flowers are purplish or bluish to almost white, resin-dotted, & are in whorls grouped in lateral & terminal clusters; the throat of the calyx is hairy; the corolla extends but little beyond the calyx. Plate 23 shows the plant before flowering. Broad-leaved (English) thyme is a variety.

Leaves, tender leafy tops, & flowering tops are used fresh or dried for flavoring various foods, including meats, fish & fish cakes, poultry, croquettes, fricassees, cheese, stews, soups, chowders, clam juice, cooked vegetables, dressings, stuffings, sauces, pickles, and vinegar. Fresh leafy sprigs are used as a garnish. An infusion of the fresh or dried leaves is said to be tonic, stimulant, carminative, antiflatulent, & antiseptic. Thyme is an ingredient of sachet & potpourri. It is an excellent source of honey & is also grown as an ornamental, often in the rock garden.

Propagation is by division, layers, cuttings, and seeds. Thyme tends to run out after several years and needs to be replaced with young plants. It is

95

adapted to rather dry, moderately light calcareous soil & full sun. In cold climates, a winter mulch is advisable, especially to prevent frost-heaving.

Thyme is native in Spain & North Africa.

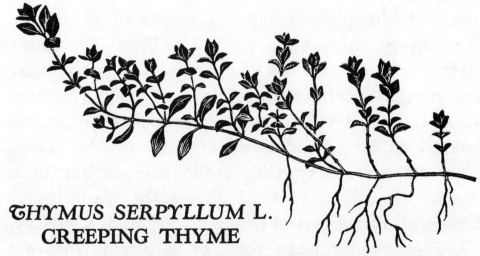

THYMUS SERPYLLUM L.
CREEPING THYME

Also called Wild Thyme, Shepherd's Thyme, Serpolet, Mother-of-Thyme, Penny Mountain, & Hillwort. French: Serpolet. German: Quendel, Feldthymian. Italian: Serpollino selvatico, Pepolino.

A LOW, creeping perennial, wild thyme forms dense mats, the older stems becoming tough & wiry. The leaves are elliptical to ovate, entire, one half inch long or less, & short-petioled. Flowers are very small, bluish or purplish, in axillary and terminal whorls or clusters, the teeth and base of the calyx hairy; the corolla extends only slightly. The plant roots at the lower nodes, the erect portion of the stems not growing more than 3 inches high. *Thymus*

96

serpyllum has many forms; variety *argenteus* & v. *aureus* have leaves variegated white and greenish-yellow respectively, the latter called golden thyme or Greek thyme; v. *citriodorus* is lemon-scented and may also be variegated (called lemon variegated or embroidered thyme, v. *citriodorus aureus*); v. *albus* is white-flowered & is called white moss thyme; red-flowered varieties are *roseus, coccineus, & splendens.*

Wild thyme has qualities similar to garden thyme and is used like it. It is one of the most effective ground covers. For making an infusion, lemon-scented thyme is considered best.

Propagation is by division, layers, cuttings, and seeds. Large mats may be divided into smaller clumps for planting. The plant is especially well-adapted to light, well-drained, calcareous soil & full sun.

It is native in Europe, temperate Asia, & North Africa & is naturalized here from southeastern Canada to North Carolina, growing as a weed in lawns, pastures, and abandoned fields.

MARRUBIUM VULGARE L. - HOARHOUND

Also Horehound. French: Marrube.
German: Weisser Andorn. Italian: Marrobio.

BRANCHED at the base, hoarhound is a clumpy, spreading perennial, reaching a height of about 2 feet, and is covered with a white, felty or woolly pubes-

PLATE 24

*Marrubium
vulgare*

cence, especially on the stems & underside of the leaves. The leaves are ovate to round, narrowing to the petiole, rugose, crenately toothed, the maximum length 2 inches. The minute white flowers are in whorls in the axils of the upper leaves; the calyx has ten teeth. A young plant is shown in Plate 24.

The plant is bitter-aromatic. An infusion of the leafy tops, fresh or dried, is reputed to be a remedy for indigestion, coughs, colds, & sore throat; it may be sweetened with honey. A candy is made by boiling sugar in a decoction of the leaves & stems. The plant is ornamental and is also attractive to bees.

Hoarhound is propagated by division, layers, cuttings, & seeds. It is best adapted to light, calcareous, rather dry soil & full sun. It may be frost-killed in cold winters. Plants should be spaced 12 inches apart.

Hoarhound is native in the temperate regions of the Old World & is naturalized throughout a large part of the United States & southern Canada.

MELISSA OFFICINALIS L. - LEMON BALM

French: Mélisse, Citronelle. German: Melisse, Citronelle, Herzkraut. Italian: Appiastro, Cedronella.

BALM IS an erect, branched, very leafy perennial, reaching a height of 2 feet or more. The leaves may reach 3 inches in length & are petioled, ovate, cre-

PLATE 25

Five times
natural size

Melissa officinalis

nate-dentate, & somewhat hairy. The flowers are in clusters in the axils of the leaves. The upper lip of the calyx has three very short lobes, & the lower has two long, spine-like divisions; the calyx is hairy. The corolla is white or yellowish-white, the tube curved upward. The plant has a lemony fragrance. Plate 25 shows a young plant & a flower.

The leaves are used, fresh or dried, for flavoring dressings, sauces, stews, soups, meats, & cooked vegetables; fresh leaves are incorporated in salads & also flavor fruit desserts, wines, liqueurs, punches, and soft drinks. A tea is prepared either by boiling or by infusion; it has been used as a domestic remedy for catarrh, influenza, & feverish colds. Balm is reputed to be carminative, diaphoretic, febrifugal, & healing when applied to wounds & infections. It is an ingredient of potpourris & is suitable for the garden border, also attractive to bees. Mr. Guzman has given the recipe of a Peruvian remedy for indigestion:

Toast a slice of bread until it is charred black. Put the charred bread & some fresh balm leaves in a cup, add boiling water, & let steep for about five minutes. Pour the liquid off, & it is ready to drink.

Propagation is by root division, layers, cuttings rooted in spring or fall, & by seeds. Seeds remain viable in storage for several years. The plant is adapted to average garden soil & is favored by partial shade.

Native in southern Europe, balm is naturalized extensively in the eastern United States.

PLATE 26

Nine times
natural size

Mentha
arvensis

MENTHA ARVENSIS L. - FIELD MINT

Also called Corn Mint & Wild Mint.
French: Baume des Champs. German: Kornminze.

FIELD MINT is a perennial, producing suckers and surface-running rootstocks. The plant is more or less erect, branched, & hairy & may be 1 to 2 feet high. Leaves are ovate to broadly lanceolate, petioled, hairy, serrate, & may reach 2 inches in length. The flowers are in axillary whorls; the calyx is hairy, gland-dotted, & has short, triangular lobes; the corolla is lilac, sometimes very pale. Variety *piperascens*, called Japanese mint, is similar, but the leaves are larger & the stems taller & strongly erect. It is used and propagated like field mint. Plate 26 shows young growth & flower of field mint. The species varies considerably in size & in degree of hairiness.

Leaves are used for flavoring like other mints but have a strong odor & taste. An infusion of the leafy tops has been used as a remedy for rheumatism and indigestion.

Propagation is by division & by cuttings. Average garden soil is suitable.

Field mint is native in Europe & temperate Asia. It is naturalized extensively in the eastern United States & is reported in some parts of the West.

Nine times
natural size

MENTHA CITRATA Ehrh. - BERGAMOT MINT

Also called Orange Mint & Lemon Mint.

A BRANCHING, stoloniferous perennial, bergamot mint is decumbent or partially so, nearly hairless, gland-dotted, & very leafy. The leaves are ovate or oval, but relatively narrower toward the top of the plant, dark green, smooth, petioled, serrate, the largest 2 inches long. Flowers are in whorls, which are axillary or in thick terminal spikes; the calyx is hairless & gland-dotted; the corolla is lavender.

The plant has a lemony odor & taste; it is used like other mints & is especially recommended for potpourri & jellies. A tea, prepared by infusion, is considered tonic & soothing.

Propagation is by division & cuttings. Moist soil and partial shade are favorable.

Bergamot mint is native in Europe & is naturalized as a wild plant in moist situations from southern New England to Missouri.

❦

MENTHA AQUATICA L. var. CRISPA Benth.

Called Curled Mint, Cross Mint, Balm Mint, Crisped-leaved Mint. French: Menthe crispée.

CURLED mint is a perennial, much branched, the stems weak & tending to sprawl. The leaves and stems are smooth, the leaves ovate, crisped, lacerate-dentate, the lower petioled & the upper sessile. The flowers are in whorls, which are in terminal spikes; the calyx is small & slightly hairy.

The plant is used for flavoring foods & beverages, its strong, piny-resinous odor recommending it for punches & julips. It is one of the best mints for the treatment of digestive ailments.

Propagation is by division & cuttings. The plant is adapted to moist soil & is found wild in wet spots from Connecticut southward. It is native in Europe.

PLATE 27

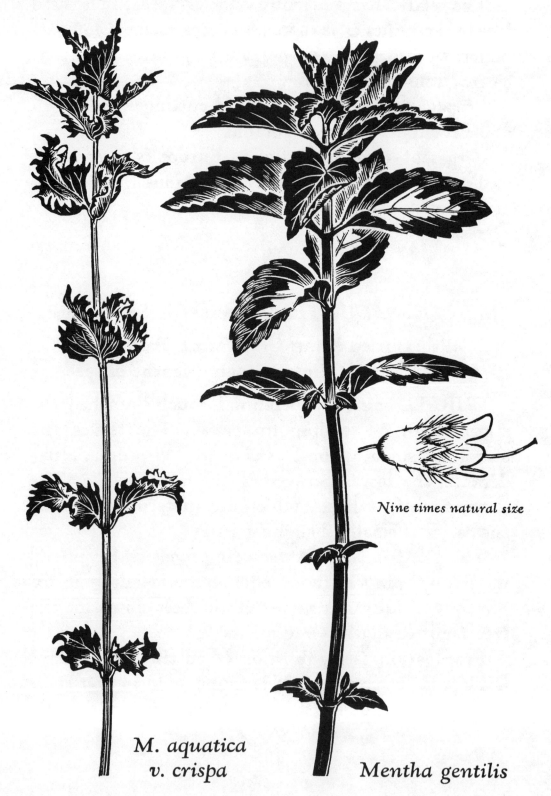

Nine times natural size

M. aquatica
v. crispa

Mentha gentilis

MENTHA GENTILIS L. - RED MINT

Also called Spotted Mint, Golden Mint, Bergamot, & Runaway Robin.

RED mint is a perennial, producing suckers; the stems are erect, nearly glabrous, dark purplish-red, and reach a height of about 2 feet. The leaves are ovate, serrate, short-stalked, dark green, often with yellowish-white blotches. The flowers are in axillary whorls. See Plate 27.

The plant is used like other mints & is propagated by division & by cuttings.

It is native in Europe & is naturalized as a wild plant from southeastern Canada to Iowa & Georgia.

MENTHA PIPERITA L. - PEPPERMINT

French: Menthe anglaise, Menthe poivrée. German: Pfefferminze. Italian: Menta pepe.

AN ERECT, branched perennial, peppermint rises from creeping rootstocks to a height of about 3 feet. Leaves are elliptical to lanceolate, nearly glabrous, serrate, gland-dotted, rather long petioled. Flowers are in thick spikes, axillary & terminal. The calyx is gland-dotted, with hairy lobes, & the corolla is pale violet. Seeds are not formed.

PLATE 28

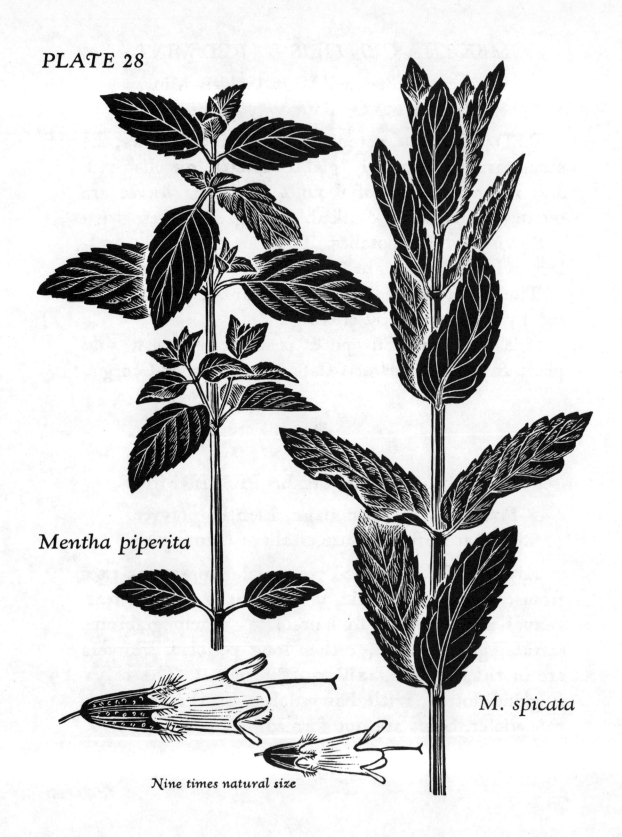

Mentha piperita

M. spicata

Nine times natural size

The leaves & flowering tops are used in flavoring foods, beverages, & candy & in the preparation of an infusion, which is aromatic & palatable & is regarded as a remedy for digestive ailments, headaches, colds, and heat exhaustion. Peppermint is grown commercially in Europe & the United States; the oil, which is extracted by distillation, is employed extensively in medicine & also in confectionery.

Plants are propagated by division & cuttings and are adapted to medium garden soil but favored by abundant moisture.

Native in Europe, peppermint has become naturalized here from southeastern Canada to Florida and Minnesota & also on the Pacific Coast. See Plate 28.

MENTHA SPICATA L. - SPEARMINT

Also called Green Mint, Roman Mint, Garden Mint. French: Menthe verte. German: Grüne Rossminze.

SPEARMINT is a perennial, producing leafy stolons. The plant is smooth, erect, & reaches a height of 2 feet. The leaves are oblong-lanceolate to ovate-lanceolate, acute, sessile, irregularly toothed, & may reach a length of more than 2 inches. The flower spikes are long & narrow, terminal & in the upper axils, the central spike exceeding the others in length. The flowers are pale violet, the calyx-teeth hairy.

Seeds are few & rarely produced. See Plate 28.

Spearmint, being very aromatic, is considered one of the best mints for flavoring. The fresh leaves and tops flavor vinegars, jellies, & iced drinks. Chopped fine, or dried & powdered, they may be added to meat & fish sauces, soups, cooked vegetables, jellies, fruit dishes, candy, ice cream & other desserts; they may be sprinkled on boiled potatoes & peas & are used to make an infusion. Spearmint is the best kind for mint sauce (chopped leaves in sweetened vinegar) which is a standard relish with cooked lamb and mutton. The plant has stimulant and carminative properties & is a remedy for nausea & flatulence.

Propagation is by division in spring, by cuttings, and by offsets. Very few seeds are produced, if any. Spearmint is adapted to average garden conditions but is favored by a moist, fertile soil. It is often infected & damaged by *Puccinia menthae* Pers., a systematic rust, which is autoecious, passing its entire life cycle in the spearmint plant. The rust is most active & evident in the spring. The vegetative parts to be used for propagation, such as cuttings, should be treated with hot water at 115 degrees Fahrenheit for ten minutes before they are planted.

Native in Europe & Asia, spearmint is extensively naturalized as a wild plant from Ontario to the Gulf of Mexico, Texas, & the Pacific Coast.

MENTHA ROTUNDIFOLIA Huds.

Called Apple Mint, Egyptian Mint, Woolly Mint.
French: Menthe crépue, Baume sauvage.
German: Rundblättrige Minze, Wilder Balsam.
Italian: Mentastro.

A PERENNIAL, apple mint grows to 2 feet or more, producing leafy stolons. The whole plant is covered with a thick, soft pubescence, which gives it a gray appearance & is slightly viscid. The leaves are roundish to elliptical, rugose, crenate-serrate, and sessile; they reach a length of 2 inches. The spikes are slender, terminal & in the upper leaf-axils. The calyx is hairy, with lanceolate-triangular teeth; the corolla is white or pink & somewhat pubescent near the lobes. See Plate 29.

The flavor is delicate, with a suggestion of apple. The hairiness of the leaves is somewhat objectionable from the culinary standpoint, but the herbage is used like other mints in meat dishes, fruit dishes, cooked vegetables, soups, sauces, jellies, desserts, apple sauce, apple pie, salads, dressings, teas and iced beverages, confectionery, & vinegar.

Propagation is by division & cuttings. Average garden conditions & moist soil are favorable.

The plant is native in Europe & is naturalized on waste ground from Maine southward.

Mentha rotundifolia Huds. var. *variegata* Hort., called pineapple mint, is similar but more slender and

grows to only 10 inches. The leaves are smaller and are variegated with irregular white patches.

Uses, propagation, & culture are the same as for apple mint. The young herbage has an aroma suggestive of pineapple, becoming more minty with age.

See the illustration on this page.

PLATE 29

*Nine times
natural size*

*Mentha
rotundifolia*

MENTHA PULEGIUM L.

Called English Pennyroyal & Pudding Grass.
French: Pouliot, Chasse-puces. German: Poleiminze.
Italian: Puleggio, Pulezzo.

ALTHOUGH pennyroyal is one of the mints, it is peculiar in its low, creeping, mat-forming habit, its susceptibility to winter-killing, strong, bitter aroma and taste, & somewhat toxic & dangerous properties. The plant is perennial, prostrate, spreading, freely branching, & rooting at the nodes. The leaves are petioled, round to oval, entire or somewhat crenate, the maximum length three quarters of an inch. The flowers are bluish, in compact axillary whorls.

The leaves have been used, fresh or dried, to flavor foods, especially puddings; the plant is more esteemed for this purpose on the continent of Europe than in Great Britain or the United States. The infusion has been used in the treatment of cramps, spasms, and colds. The plant contains a somewhat toxic essential oil; it must be used with caution & in small amounts.

It is propagated by division in fall or spring, by seeds, & sometimes by cuttings; the plant is adapted to fertile, moist soil & partial shade.

It is native in Europe & adjacent Asia & is reported as occurring wild in California.

Hedeoma pulegioides, American pennyroyal, is an erect annual, strongly resembling the English kind in flavor. Plate 30 shows English pennyroyal.

PLATE 30

Nine times natural size

Mentha pulegium

MONARDA DIDYMA L. - BEE BALM

Also called Oswego Tea, Bergamot, Red Balm, American Melissa, Horse Mint, & Indian's Plume.

A CLUMP-forming perennial, bee balm reaches a height of 3 feet or more. The roots are creeping, the stems erect, acutely four-angled, and rather hairy. Leaves are petioled, ovate, acuminate, serrate, hairy, reaching a length of 5 to 6 inches; their odor is pungent & lemony. Flowers are in dense terminal clusters, which are subtended by reddish bracts. The corolla is smooth or finely pubescent, & its typical color is scarlet-red, although it ranges in horticultural forms through rose, salmon, cherry, & purple.

An aromatic tea is prepared from the leaves by boiling or infusion. The leaves are used for flavoring wine & fruit cups, fruit salad, & apple jelly. The plant is often raised as an ornamental.

It is propagated by dividing the clumps in spring and may also be started from seeds; it is adapted to average garden conditions but favored by moisture.

Native in eastern North America, bee balm ranges from southern Canada to Tennessee & Georgia. It was introduced into Europe as an ornamental in 1754.

The top of a flowering plant is shown in Plate 31.

Monarda fistulosa L., called wild bergamot and Oswego tea, is similar, but the stems are more slender and are obtusely four-angled. The leaves are ovate to lanceolate, the largest 4 inches long. The flowers are

PLATE 31

Monarda didyma

smaller than those of the preceding species & are in dense clusters, which are terminal & in the upper leaf-axils; the bracts subtending the clusters are purplish or white. The corolla is pink, lilac, lavender, or purple, the upper lip very hairy. There is a variety with white flowers.

Uses are the same as for bee balm. Both species were used medicinally by the American Indians.

Propagation & culture of wild bergamot are the same as for bee balm, but the former is more tolerant of dryish soil.

It is also native in North America, ranging from Maine to Minnesota & south to the Gulf of Mexico.

Monarda punctata L. has a yellow corolla with purple spots. It is also native in North America.

❦

NEPETA CATARIA L. - CATNIP or CATMINT

French: Chataire, Herbe aux Chats.
German: Katzenminze. Italian: Erba gatta, Gattaja.

A BRANCHING, erect perennial, catnip grows to a height of 3 feet and is covered with a downy pubescence, which gives the plant a grayish appearance. The leaves are ovate, heart-shaped at the base, petioled, coarsely crenate-toothed, & 2 to 3 inches long. The flowers are in close clusters, which are in compact spikes at the ends of the stems & branches. The

118

calyx is very hairy, with narrow, pointed teeth; the corolla is white or faintly tinged with violet & has violet dots; it extends but little beyond the calyx; the upper lip is erect. The plant has a characteristic odor, not altogether pleasant.

Although strongly flavored, the leaves and shoots have been used to flavor sauces & cooked foods, the dried leaves used in herb mixtures for soups & stews, and the flowering tops & leaves to prepare a tea. The infusion is reputed to be sedative & soporific and a remedy for fevers, colds, & flatulence; it is emetic in large doses. Catnip is attractive to bees. It is considered a tonic for cats & is sold in packages in pet shops for this purpose. In harvesting catnip, the flowering heads & tender herbage are cut off, shade-dried, stripped & crumbled by hand-rubbing, and stored in jars.

Propagation is by root division in spring or by seeds sown preferably in the fall; germination is usually prompt; seeds remain viable in storage several years. The plant thrives in average garden soil and self-sows. It has become a common dooryard weed in the northern United States.

Catnip is native in Europe & temperate Asia. Its range here is from southern Canada to Georgia and westward to Oregon.

Several other species of *Nepeta* are cultivated, for ornament or ground cover mainly, although they are also aromatic.

PLATE 32

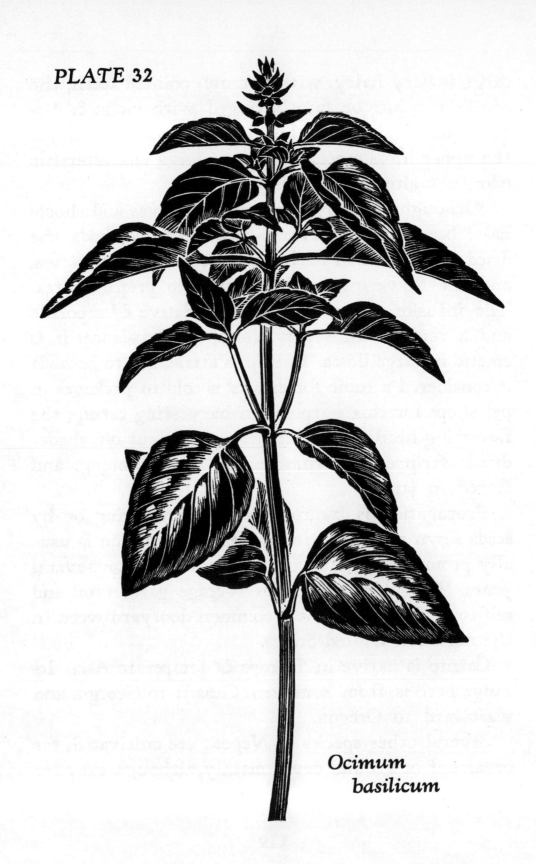

Ocimum
basilicum

OCIMUM BASILICUM L. - SWEET BASIL

French: Basilie, Herbe Royale. Italian: Basilico.
German: Basilie, Königskraut.

AN ERECT annual, basil is profusely branched, smooth, and reaches 2 feet, sometimes more. Leaves may reach 2 inches in length & are stalked, ovate, entire or with small teeth, smooth, almost glossy, dark green. Flowers are white or purplish-white, in whorls of about six, the whorls racemed. The plant has a clove-like scent & spicy flavor. Plate 32 shows the top of a plant before blooming. The varieties of sweet basil include a purple-leaved one, a curled-leaved one, which may be either green or purple, and one with a lemony scent.

One of the most useful & popular culinary herbs, basil is used, fresh or dried, for flavoring meat, fish, egg, & cheese dishes; it is incorporated in ox-tail and mock turtle soup & others, also in stews, sausage, dressings, sauces, & salads; it is used with all tomato dishes, especially with spaghetti, & is sprinkled on boiled potatoes & peas, & flavors vinegar, tomato juice, vegetable juice cocktails, & fruit beverages. A boiling-water infusion may be made, the herbage being considered stimulant, cooling, nervine, & carminative. The plant is also grown as an ornamental.

Basil is propagated by seeds, which germinate in four or five days; they remain viable in storage for several years. The plants are adapted to average gar-

121

den soil & full sun exposure & may be spaced 12 to 18 inches apart. Cutting back stimulates new growth. Plants may be grown in pots indoors in winter.

Basil is native in the tropical regions of Asia and Africa & occurs wild on the islands of the Pacific. It has been grown in India since ancient times, being sacred to Vishnu in the Hindu religion.

Ocimum minimum L., called bush basil, is similar to sweet basil but is smaller in all of its parts & is more compact & bush-like. The stems do not grow over 10 inches high. The leaves reach a maximum length of a half inch. A very small form with leaves a quarter of an inch long is known as dwarf basil. Bush basil & dwarf basil may have either green or purple foliage. Both are spicy-flavored & are culti-vated, harvested, & used like sweet basil. They may be used as border plants for flower & herb beds.

ROSMARINUS OFFICINALIS L. - ROSEMARY
French: Romarin. German: Rosmarin, Kranzenkraut. Italian: Ramerino, Rosmarino.

ROSEMARY is an evergreen, half-hardy peren-nial shrub, grown in the North as an annual. In mild climates it reaches a height of 4 or 5 feet. The leaves are narrow, revolute-margined, entire, dotted, green above & gray-hairy beneath, sessile, the length

PLATE 33

Rosmarinus
officinalis

reaching an inch & a half. The flowers are bluish, and are in short, axillary racemes. The herbage has a pungent, resinous flavor. See Plate 33.

The fresh, tender tops are used for garnishing and for flavoring cold drinks, pickles, soups, and other foods. The leaves, chopped fresh or dried & powdered, are added to cooked meats, fish, poultry, soups, stews, sauces, dressings, preserves, & jams; they are employed as a condiment with peas, potatoes, and other vegetables, & with salt meats, & are mixed with sage in pork & veal stuffings & sometimes are put into biscuits. A tea prepared from the leaves is reputed to be remedial for nervous ailments & headaches. The dried leaves are smoked for the relief of asthma & are incorporated in sachets & potpourris. Oil of rosemary is used commercially in perfumes, hair tonics, and medicine. The plant is often cultivated as an ornamental.

Harvesting is done by picking the leaves from the branches when the plants are in bloom. The leaves are then spread out & dried in the shade.

Propagation is by division, cuttings, layers, & seeds. Cuttings root readily, but seeds are slow to germinate, requiring several weeks; they may be started early indoors. Rosemary is adapted to light, dry, calcareous soil & full sun. Plants may be spaced 2 or 3 feet apart; they may be cool-stored indoors in winter.

Rosemary is native on the coast of the Mediterranean Sea & in the adjacent hilly regions.

SALVIA OFFICINALIS L. - SAGE

French: Sauge, Serve. German: Garten-Salbei.
Italian: Salvia, Erba Savia.

A SMALL, gray-green, perennial shrub, sage has erect, stiff stems 1 to 2 feet high. Leaves are stalked, elliptical to oblong, the tips usually rounded, margins entire or crenulate, the surface covered with small pebbly nodules, length 1 to 3 inches. Flowers are bluish or purplish, in racemed whorls, the racemes in the upper leaf-axils. The bell-shaped calyx has sharp, narrow teeth, the two lower exceeding the others; hairs are present in the corolla. Sage is shown in Plate 34. There are several varieties of sage, one with red foliage, others variegated; one has white flowers; some horticulturists recognize broad- and narrow-leaved varieties. One of the most practical is "Holt's Mammoth", which is large & vigorous in vegetative growth.

The fresh leaves, which have an aromatic, bitterish flavor, are chopped & used to flavor cheese, pickles, and sausage; dried & powdered, they are commonly incorporated in poultry & pork stuffings & bologna sausage; they are mixed with cooked vegetables, such as tomatoes & snap beans, sprinkled on cheese dishes, fish, pork, & other cooked meats. Sage is thought to be an aid in digesting fat. In old times the Christmas boar's head was cooked in vinegar & water to which were added sage, thyme, & rosemary. Sage tea, pre-

125

PLATE 34

Salvia officinalis

pared by infusion of a teaspoonful of fresh or dried leaves to a cup of water, is warming in effect and agreeable to the taste; although used as a home remedy for various disorders, its medicinal properties are probably feeble. *Salvia officinalis* and several other species of sage are grown for ornamental purposes.

Plants are propagated by division, layers, cuttings, and seeds. The first three are the best methods, since strains with desirable qualities often do not come true to seed. Herbaceous cuttings root readily. Plants gradually become too woody & should be renewed every three or four years. They are adapted to average garden soil & full sun & respond to cultivation and applications of fertilizer. They need abundant space & should be set 18 to 24 inches apart.

Sage is native in the Mediterranean region.

SALVIA SCLAREA L. - CLARY

French: Sclarée, Toute Bonne. German: Scharlach, Römische Salbei, Muskatellerkraut. Italian: Sclarea, Scarleggia, Erba Moscadella, Herba San Giovanni.

CLARY is biennial and herbaceous, producing a clump of radical leaves the first year & a flowering stalk, reaching 3 feet or more, the second year. The plant is pubescent & viscid. Basal leaves are large and broad-bladed, petioled, ovate, cordate, rugose, pu-

PLATE 35

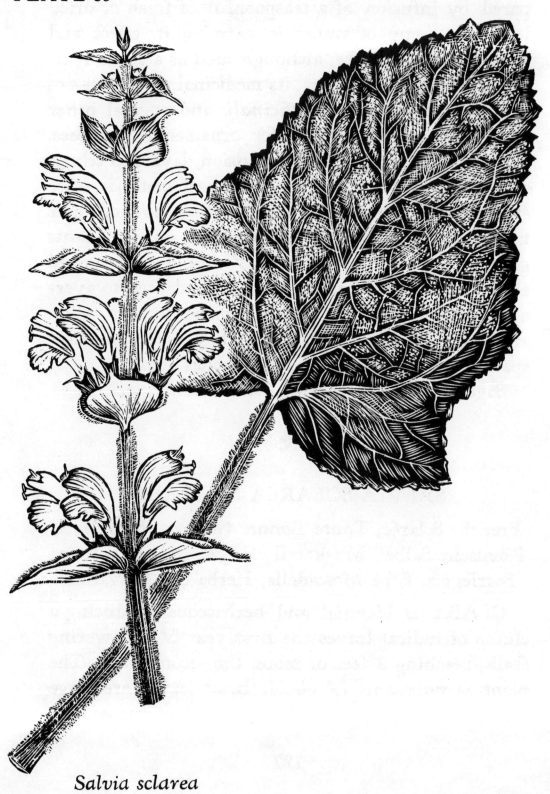

Salvia sclarea

bescent, margins irregularly crenate or denticulate; upper leaves are similar but much smaller and are short-petioled to sessile. Flowers are white, pale blue to purplish-blue, & dull pink; they are in whorls subtended by whitish or pinkish, leafy bracts, the whorls arranged in loose axillary & terminal spikes. The plant has a somewhat lavender-like odor. Clary is shown in Plate 35.

The leaves, fresh or dried, are sometimes used for flavoring & seasoning like common sage. They have been used to adulterate the flavor of Rhine wine to resemble muscatel; they may be used to flavor omelettes; dried, they are incorporated in sachets & potpourris. A tea is prepared from the flowers. The seeds provide a mucilaginous drink reputed to be a remedy for heat prostration. The plant has ornamental value.

The leaves, being larger than those of most herbs, are easily picked by hand separately. They should be spread out in a single layer, dried thoroughly, and crumbled by hand-rubbing. Since clary is biennial, leaves may be harvested from the same plant during two growing periods, starting in midsummer the first season, & ending about then in the second year.

Clary is propagated by seeds sown in spring; it often self-sows. Average garden conditions are suitable; spacing may be about 18 inches apart.

Clary is native in southern Europe & the Mediterranean region. It is naturalized here from Pennsylvania to South Carolina.

SATUREJA HORTENSIS L.-SUMMER SAVORY

French: Sarriette, Savourée. German: Bohnenkraut, Pfefferkraut. Italian: Savoreggia, Santoreggia.

AN ERECT, bushy annual, much branched but compact, summer savory may reach a height of 18 inches. The stems are hairy. The leaves are sessile or short-stalked, oblong-linear, acute at the apex, about an inch long, the margins entire. Flowers are small, pink-white, blue-white, or purple-white, in terminal and axillary whorls or clusters; the calyx is dotted and sharp-toothed, the corolla & stamens only slightly exserted. Summer savory & winter savory closely resemble each other, but the latter has hairless stems, which become woody below.

One of the best culinary herbs, summer savory, when rubbed on meat before cooking, brings out or imparts a rich flavor; the leaves are also used to flavor poultry, egg & vegetable dishes, croquettes, sausage, scrambled eggs, & sometimes cakes & puddings; they are recommended in soups, stews, sauces, dressings, stuffings, & gravies. Dried, pulverized leaves are usually used, but fresh sprigs may be added to salad, boiled with beans or peas, & used as a garnish. A tea is prepared from fresh or dried leaves & is said to be expectorant & carminative. Savory is a bee-plant & an ornamental.

Propagation is by seeds sown in spring. The plant self-sows readily & responds to average garden soil and full sun, but will grow on drier & poorer soils. Spacing should be about 12 inches apart.

Summer savory is native in the Mediterranean region. It is naturalized from southeastern Canada to Kentucky & Nevada, especially in dry, barren places.

❧

SATUREJA MONTANA L. - WINTER SAVORY

French: Sarriette. German: Winterbohnenkraut, Karst-Saturei. Italian: Santoreggia.

A SMALL, evergreen, perennial semishrub, winter savory is woody below, branching, erect, & grows to 18 inches. Leaves are linear to oblong-linear, acute, sessile, about 1 inch long, slightly hairy, the margins entire; the leaves are persistent. Flowers are small, white to pink-white & purple-white, in whorls arranged in racemes or panicles; the calyx is dotted and has acuminate teeth; the corolla is dotted and only slightly exserted. See Plate 36.

Of slightly stronger flavor than the preceding species, winter savory is used like it to flavor poultry, meat, eggs, sausage, vegetables, stuffings, dressings, sauces, gravies, soups, stews, cakes, & puddings. The leaves are put into salad & are used to make a tea, which is said to be carminative. The plant is attractive to bees & suitable for flower garden or rockery.

It is propagated by seeds or by division, layers, and

131

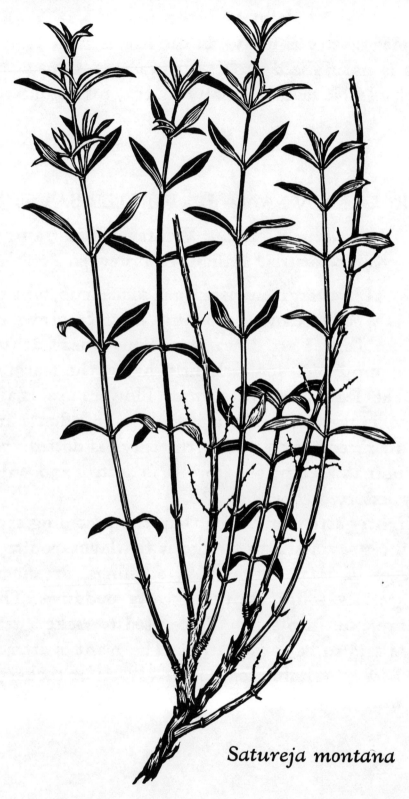

Satureja montana

cuttings; the latter are made from the side branches in spring; the plant often self-sows. Winter savory is adapted to light, dryish soil & full sun.

It is native in the Mediterranean region.

❦

CUNILA ORIGANOIDES (L.) Britt. - DITTANY

Also called Maryland Dittany & Stone-mint.

A LOW perennial, Maryland dittany has tufted, much-branched stems, not more than 16 inches high. The leaves are ovate, acute, rounded at the base, nearly sessile, smooth, gland-dotted, about 1 inch long, margins sparsely toothed. Flowers are white, pinkish, or purplish, in rounded clusters at the ends of the branches & in the axils. The calyx is hairy in the throat & has five equal lobes; the corolla is bilabiate, the tube exserted, the upper lip erect.

The plant has a minty flavor & is used to make a mildly stimulating tea. It is much grown as an ornamental border subject.

An American species, stone-mint is found wild in dry woods from New York to Indiana & southward to Florida & Texas.

PLATE 37

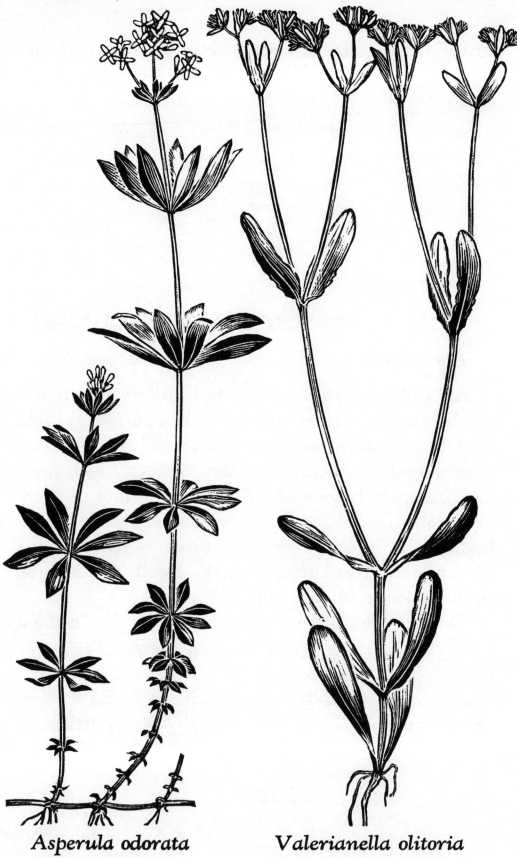

Asperula odorata   *Valerianella olitoria*

ℭ RUBIACEAE ⋅ MADDER FAMILY

WOODY OR herbaceous plants, the members of this family have simple, opposite or whorled leaves, & usually perfect and regular flowers. The petals are united into a four- or five-lobed corolla. The stamens are equal in number to the lobes of the corolla & are attached to the tube. The ovary is inferior. Most of the members are tropical plants, for example, coffee, cinchona (quinine), madder, & gardenia. The bedstraws are European or Asian plants.

ASPERULA ODORATA L. ⋅ SWEET WOODRUFF

Also called Rockweed, Hay-plant, Mugget, Woodrip,
Star Grass, Sweet Grass, Sweet Hairhoof.
French: Aspérule odorante, Petit Muguet.
German: Waldmeister. Italian: Asperella odorata.

AN ERECT perennial, reaching only 8 or 10 inches in height, sweet woodruff has oblong-lanceolate leaves arranged in whorls, each whorl with about 8 leaves. The flowers are white, in terminal & axillary cymes; the corolla is four-lobed. The fruit is globose and hispid. Sweet woodruff is a coumarin-containing plant, hay-scented when dried. See Plate 37.

The fresh herb is used to flavor cold drinks and wine & is boiled to make a tea, which is reputed to be cordial, stomachic, tonic, diuretic, & pectoral. The dried leaves are used sparingly to flavor punch, tea, and other beverages & are added to potpourris and used to perfume linens. The plant is often grown as an ornamental ground cover & border subject. The German *Maibowle* is made of Rhine wine flavored with sprigs of woodruff picked before blooming.

Propagation is usually by root division in spring. Pieces of the runners, with roots & shoots starting at the joints, are cut off & set about a foot apart in rows. Seeds are slow to germinate & are best planted in summer as soon as ripe. The flavor & growth of the plants are improved by full or partial shade and moist soil.

Sweet woodruff is native in Europe.

❴ VALERIANACEAE ⸱ VALERIAN FAMILY

THE PLANTS of this family are mostly herbaceous & grow chiefly in the northern hemisphere. The leaves are opposite, the inflorescence more or less cymose. The corolla is tubular & five-lobed. One to three stamens are present, attached to the tube of the corolla; the calyx is adherent to the ovary.

VALERIANELLA OLITORIA Poll.

Called Corn Salad, Lamb's Lettuce, Milk Grass,
White Pot-herb, Field Salad, & Mache.
French: Valérianelle, Mâche, Blanchette, Doucette.
German: Gemeiner Feldsalat. Italian: Dolcetta,
Morbidello, Cecerello, Aguellino, Saleggia.

CORN SALAD is an annual or winter annual, dichotomously branching near the base, mostly glabrous, & producing a basal cluster or rosette of leaves. The plant reaches a height of 12 inches. Leaves are spatulate to oblong-lanceolate, the lower entire, the upper somewhat dentate. The flowers are blue, in small, compact cymes with short peduncles. The fruit is roundish in outline but somewhat flattened, the seed-bearing locule having a corky thickening at the back. Corn salad is shown in Plate 37.

The leaves may be used alone for salad or mixed with other greens; they are also cooked as a pot-herb.

Propagation is by seeds, which ripen in April or May or later, & may be sown the same season. As a winter annual, the plant makes its initial growth in the fall & flowers in the spring; growth is checked by hot weather.

The species is naturalized from Europe. It occurs in waste places and as a field weed from Maine to Idaho, Louisiana & northeastward.

There are several other wild species similar in appearance but white-flowered.

137

PLATE 38

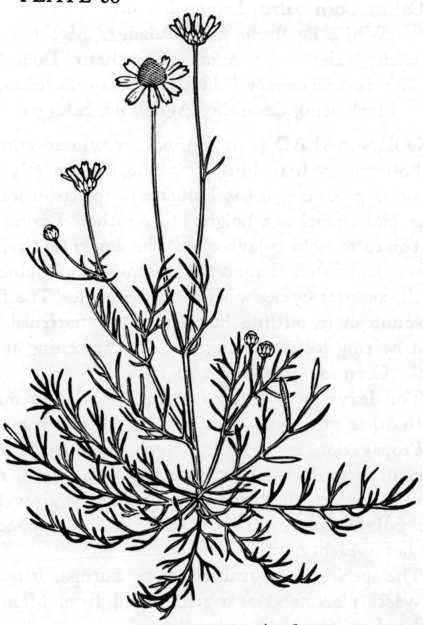

Anthemis nobilis

ℂ *COMPOSITAE* · COMPOSITE FAMILY

THE LARGEST family of the seed-bearing plants, the *Compositae* consist principally of herbaceous plants with the flowers borne in a compact head on a common receptacle subtended by an involucre. The corolla is tubular or ligulate, four- or five-lobed; the stamens are four or five in number & are borne on the corolla tube, the filaments separate, the anthers united in a ring. Flowers with a ligulate corolla are ray-flowers; those with a tubular corolla are disk-flowers. The scales borne on the receptacle among the flowers are called the chaff; those which subtend the whole head are the bracts. The fruit is typically an achene, which may be surmounted with a crown of scales, bristles, or hairs. Some cultivated ornamentals of the family are zinnia, dahlia, chrysanthemum, and sunflower. Many members are common weeds.

ANTHEMIS NOBILIS L.

Called Roman Chamomile, Garden Chamomile, English Chamomile, Low Chamomile, Ground Apple. French: Camomille. German: Kamille.

A LOW, almost trailing perennial, less than a foot high, Roman chamomile has finely dissected, alternate leaves & is covered with a downy pubescence.

The flower heads are nearly 1 inch in diameter, the disk yellow, the rays white; the receptacle is rounded to cone-shaped; chaff is present & is blunt at the tip. There is a form with double ray florets, which is less vigorous in growth; the form with single rays is preferred because of the larger disks, since the disk-flowers have a greater concentration of the medicinal principle. A plant is shown in Plate 38.

An infusion of the dried flowers provides a refreshing tea & is made by pouring one pint of boiling water on one half ounce of flowers, & letting them steep for ten minutes; the liquid is strained, and honey, sugar, milk, or cream may be added. The tea is considered to be tonic, stomachic, carminative, and sedative & is a home remedy for indigestion and feverish colds. The oil is used officially in medicine.

Propagation is by seeds, division of the roots in spring or fall, stem cuttings, & layering of the runners. Germination is prompt. Mature plants should be spaced 6 inches apart. A light, dry soil & full sun exposure are most favorable.

The flower heads are harvested at the height of bloom. Their gathering is a tedious process; they are best cut off with scissors; when pulled off, too much stem & leaf material comes off with them. The heads should be spread out in a thin layer & thoroughly dried in the shade. They are stored in tight glass jars.

Chamomile is native in southern and western Europe. It is occasionally found here as an escape.

MATRICARIA CHAMOMILLA L.
GERMAN CHAMOMILE

French: Camomille vraie. German: Echte Kamille.
Italian: Camomilla, Capomilla.

A SMOOTH, upright, branching annual, German chamomile reaches a height of 15 inches or more. It has alternate leaves, pinnately dissected two to three times, the ultimate segments very narrow. The heads have yellow disks & white rays & are mostly in terminal inflorescences; each head is nearly 1 inch in diameter. At an advanced stage of bloom the rays are reflexed, & the receptacle becomes elongate and hollow; it is not chaffy. Vigorous & free-flowering, the plants tend to become weedy.

An aromatic tea is prepared by infusion of the dried heads, steeped for ten minutes in boiling water. It is reputed to have properties similar to those of Roman chamomile. A diluted tincture of the heads has been used on the skin to repel insects.

Propagation is by seeds, which germinate readily and often self-sow. The plant is adapted to light, dry soil & full sun.

It is native in Europe & in the temperate zone of Asia. It is reported as growing wild in this country in southern New York & Pennsylvania.

PLATE 39

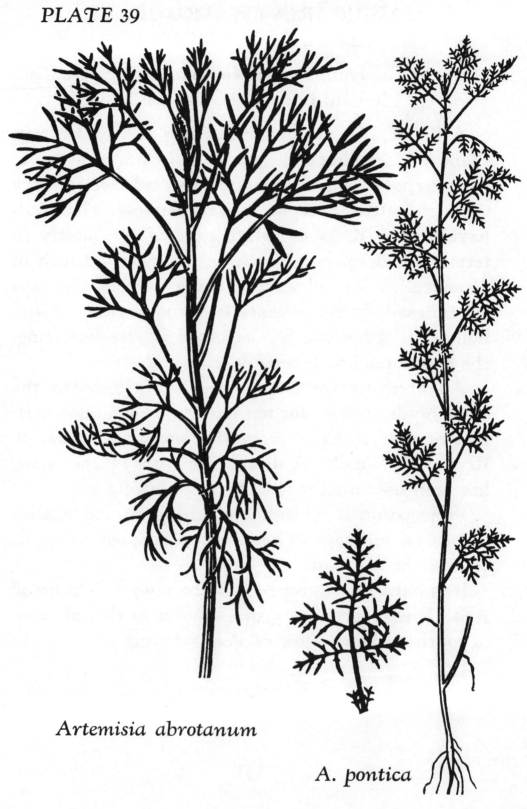

Artemisia abrotanum

A. pontica

ARTEMISIA ABROTANUM L.
SOUTHERNWOOD

Also called Old Man, Lad's Love, Sweet Benjamin,
Slovenwood, & Gardenrobe.
French: Abrotone, Citronelle, Garde Robe.
German: Eberraute, Stabwurz. Italian: Abrotono.

A SHRUBBY perennial, with a rather erect habit
of growth, southernwood has finely divided, alternate leaves & small, yellow-white flower heads in
loose panicles. The whole plant is gray-green & may
reach 3 to 5 feet in height. It has an aromatic and
lemony fragrance. There is a dwarf form of southernwood, which reaches only 18 inches. Southernwood is shown in Plate 39.

The young shoots are used to flavor cakes and
puddings. A tea is made from the flowers & herbage
by infusion; boiling is not desirable. The leaves are
said to be moth-repellent and have also been used
medicinally in poultices & as a stimulant, astringent,
antiseptic, anthelmintic, & deobstruent. The plant is
frequently grown for ornamental purposes.

Propagation is by root division and by cuttings,
which root readily. Plants may be spaced 3 to 4 feet
apart; they respond to good garden soil & full sun.

Southernwood has been introduced from Europe,
where it is native in the Mediterranean region; it
is found wild in this country on waste ground from
Massachusetts to Nebraska.

PLATE 40

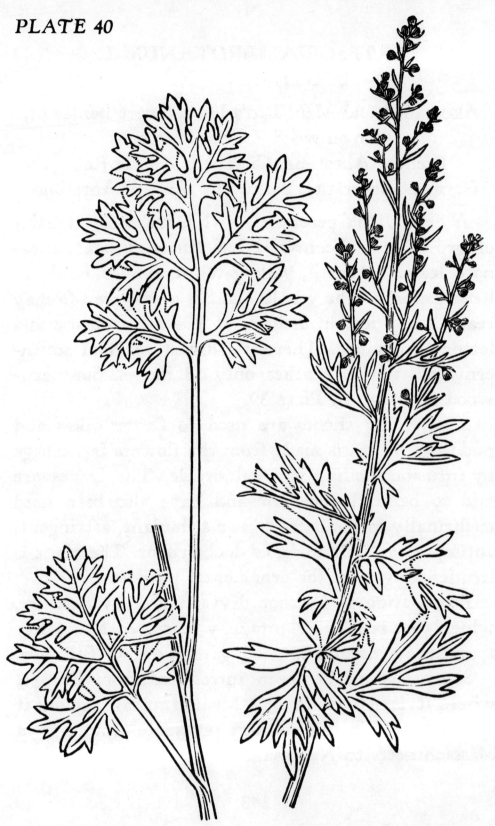

Artemisia absinthium

ARTEMISIA ABSINTHIUM L. - WORMWOOD

Also called Absinth. French: Absinthe.
German: Wermut, Absinth. Italian: Assenzio.

AN EXPANSIVE, spreading, shrub-like perennial, wormwood may grow to 4 feet. It has coarsely lobed, alternate leaves, which are covered with a silky pubescence, giving the plant a gray appearance. The flower-heads are hemispherical & are borne in panicles. See Plate 40.

The leafy tops have been placed on roast goose in the oven to cut the grease. A decoction of the leaves and flowers is used medicinally for colds, fevers, poor digestion, & rheumatism; it is considered to be tonic, anthelmintic, antiseptic, stomachic, & antiflatulent. The volatile oil distilled from *Artemisia absinthium* is the main ingredient of the French liqueur, absinth. Wormwood has ornamental value in the garden.

Propagation is by cuttings, root division, & seeds. Germination is slow. The plants are favored by a soil which contains some clay. Stakes are sometimes used to hold the plants more upright.

Harvesting is done when the plants are in full bloom. The less woody stems & branches, with their flowering tops, should be cut off and dried in the shade, then stripped, pulverized, & stored.

The plant has been naturalized from Europe and occurs wild on this continent from Newfoundland to northern New England.

PLATE 41

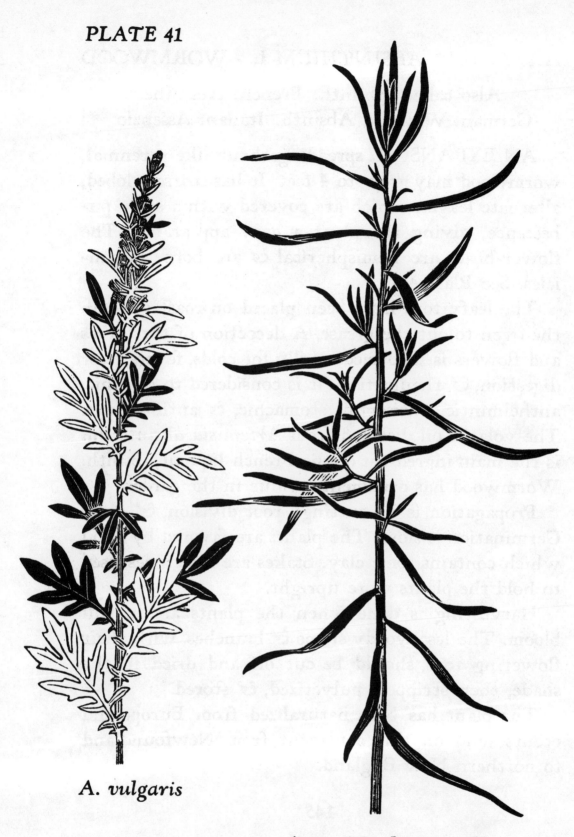

A. vulgaris

Artemisia dracunculus

ARTEMISIA DRACUNCULUS L. - TARRAGON

French: Eſtragon. German: Dragon, Escadronkraut.
Italian: Dragone, Eſtragon, Dragoncello.

TARRAGON is perennial and herbaceous but is somewhat shrub-like in growth, tending to be woody at the base. The leaves are alternate, long & narrow, with entire margins. The small, greenish-white flower heads are in loose panicles. The plant reaches a height of about 2 feet. See Plate 41.

The fresh leaves are used in pickles & salads and for flavoring vinegar. Dried, they are added to chops, ſteaks, soups, ſtews, egg dishes, chicken, mushrooms, tartar sauce, fish sauces, cream sauces, muſtard, preserves, & mayonnaise. To make tarragon vinegar, fill a jar loosely with fresh leaves and add enough vinegar to cover them. Let this ſtand three weeks, then strain it into a fresh jar or bottle. White vinegar, particularly wine vinegar, is preferable.

Two harvestings of the leaves may be made in the same season, the firſt in midsummer, the second in late summer or early fall, before frost occurs. The leafy stems are cut, spread out or hung up in small bunches to dry, & then stripped & stored.

Propagation is by cuttings from the ſtem & root. Seeds are seldom produced. Although fairly hardy, the plants may require winter protection in northern climates. Dry soil & a sunny exposure are beſt.

Tarragon is native in southern Russia.

PLATE 42

Carthamus tinctorius

ARTEMISIA VULGARIS L. - MUGWORT

Also called Felon Herb, St. John's Plant, Bulwand, Sailor's Tobacco, & Green Ginger.
French: Armoise, Couronne de St. Jean, Tabac de St. Pierre. German: Beifuss, Fliegenkraut.
Italian: Amarella, Assenzio selvatico, Canapaccia.

A PERENNIAL, mugwort grows from stout rhizomes or rootstocks to a height of 3 feet or more; it is erect & branching, the stems often purplish. The mature leaves are dark green above, but the underside is white with a cottony pubescence. The leaves are cleft into lanceolate lobes, the upper leaves becoming narrow or linear. The flower-heads are very small, numerous, light yellow, in paniculate spikes. See Plate 41. A white-flowered variety (v. *lactiflora*) is grown as an ornamental & is usually listed in the trade as *Artemisia lactiflora*, called white mugwort or ghostplant wormwood. Golden-leaved and variegated forms are known.

The dried leaves are put into stuffing for roast goose. Infusions of the leaves & rootstocks are used medicinally to ward off colds, relieve indigestion, and stimulate the appetite. The flowering tops, dried and powdered, are utilized in the same way. The herbage is reputed to be moth-repellent.

Propagation is by division. The plant responds to good soil & culture but is able to withstand drouth and other unfavorable conditions. Leaves & tops are

149

cut & dried in August; rootstocks are dug in the fall, thoroughly washed, & dried whole.

Mugwort is native to Europe, Asia, & northern and western North America. It is widely distributed in the United States, where it has become a weed of pastures & fields.

ARTEMISIA PONTICA L.
ROMAN WORMWOOD

French: Petite Absinthe.
German: Römischer Wermuth, Gartenzypresse.

ROMAN wormwood is a perennial, gray, shrubby plant, with finely dissected, alternate leaves & small pale yellow flower-heads in long panicles. It reaches a height of 2 feet. Plate 39 shows a leafy stem and a single larger leaf.

A decoction of the leaves & flowers is used for colds, as a tonic, & as an anthelmintic; the leafy top is a bitter stomachic & induces perspiration. Roman wormwood is an ingredient of vermouth. It is milder in its properties than common wormwood. It is often grown as an ornamental for its gray effect.

Propagation is by cuttings, root division, & some-times by seeds, although germination is slow.

Native to central Europe, the plant is naturalized here from Massachusetts to New Jersey & westward.

CARTHAMUS TINCTORIUS L. - SAFFLOWER

Also called American Saffron, Saffron-thistle,
False Saffron, Dyer's Saffron.
French: Safranon, Safre, Safran bâtard.
German: Falscher Safran, Färber-Saflor.
Italian: Cartamo, Zaffrone, Scardiccione, Attrattile.

AN ERECT annual, safflower may reach a height
of 3 feet, the stem branching near the top. Leaves
are dark green, glossy, alternate, ovate-lanceolate, the
upper ones clasping; the margins are spinose. Flower-
heads are bright orange & may be over an inch in
diameter. Plate 42 shows a flowering top.

The principal adulterant & substitute for saffron,
safflower is also used in the cosmetic industry for
making rouge. It was formerly used in dyeing tex-
tiles, but is now largely replaced by cheaper & more
permanent artificial dyes. It is used to color butter
and margarine. In India, the oil extracted from the
seeds is used in cooking. The plant is cultivated to a
considerable extent in India, Egypt, & China. Here
and in Europe safflower is also cultivated for ornamental purposes. In the manufacture of rouge, the
flowers are washed, dried, powdered, & put through
a chemical process, which precipitates the coloring
principle, carthamin, as a red powder; this is then
mixed with powdered talc.

Average garden soil & full sun favor growth.
Carthamus tinctorius is native in the East Indies.

PLATE 43

Tanacetum vulgare

TANACETUM VULGARE L. - TANSY

Also called Cow Bitters & Button Bitters.
French: Tanaisie, Herbe aux Vers, Herbe St. Marc.
German: Rainfarn, Wurmkraut. Italian: Tanaceto.

TANSY is a perennial, its erect, unbranched stems forming clumps & often reaching 3 feet in height. Leaves are alternate & pinnately divided into oblong, pointed segments which are cut or incised into secondary, serrate lobes; the lower leaves may be a foot long. Flowers are yellow, tubular, the marginal ones with three-toothed, upright rays; the heads are clustered in flat-topped corymbs. Variety *crispum*, or fern-leaved tansy, is a horticultural form. An older name of tansy was *Chrysanthemum vulgare*. Leaves and flowers are shown in Plate 43.

An old-time herb, tansy is little used now, but young, tender leaves, chopped fine, may be used in small amounts to flavor omelettes, stews, puddings, cakes, cheese, & salads. A tea is also made from them; it is said to be tonic, diaphoretic, & anthelmintic. The herbage contains a toxic oil & probably should not be eaten. In large doses, tansy tea acts as an irritant narcotic & has been cited as a cause of death.

Propagation is by division & by seeds, which self-sow. The plant spreads freely from creeping roots and needs liberal space; the stems may lodge & need staking. Average soil & full sun are favorable.

Tansy is native in Europe & naturalized here.

PLATE 44

Chrysanthemum
balsamita

CHRYSANTHEMUM BALSAMITA L.

Called Costmary, Sweet Mary, Bible Leaf, Alecost.
French: Menthe de Notre Dame, Menthe romaine.
German: Marienblatt, Bibelblatt, Marienbalsam.
Italian: Erba Santa Maria, Erba Costa, Maria Santa.

A PERENNIAL, costmary spreads from the underground parts & forms large clumps; the stiff, erect stems may reach a height of 4 feet; they have numerous short branches & are slightly downy. The leaves are alternate, oval, lobed near the base, the largest over 6 inches long; the margins are crenate. The flower-heads are small, yellow, & have several white ray-flowers. Variety *tanacetoides* has rayless heads. Plate 44 shows a leafy top & a large leaf.

The leaves have a sweet, minty, lemony flavor, and are used fresh like mint for flavoring tea and iced drinks; dried, they are used to make an infusion. Linens are perfumed with dried costmary, with or without an admixture of lavender. The plant was used in medieval times for flavoring ale & beer. It is suitable for the garden border but tends to become sprawly or straggly late in the season.

Costmary is propagated by division and by root cuttings. Seeds are seldom produced. Dry soil & full sun prove best to promote flowering, but some shade is tolerated. A generous spacing, 3 to 4 feet, should be provided.

Costmary is native in western Asia.

155

PLATE 45

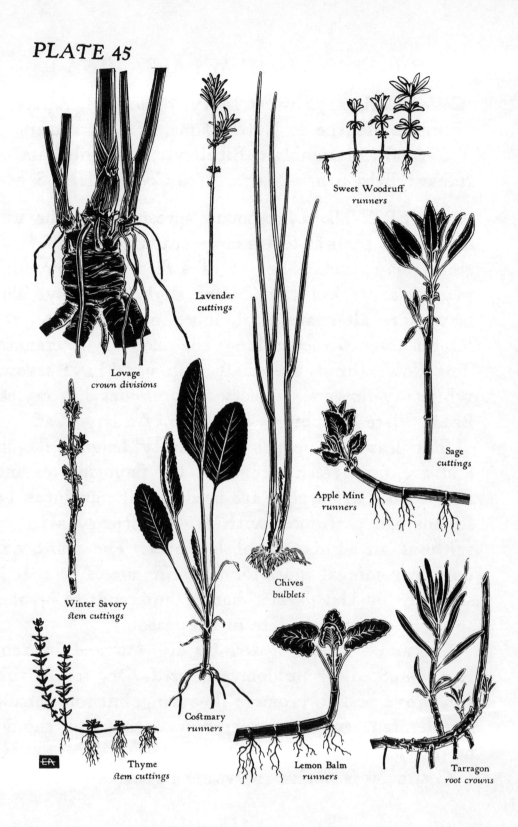

Lovage
crown divisions

Lavender
cuttings

Sweet Woodruff
runners

Sage
cuttings

Winter Savory
stem cuttings

Costmary
runners

Chives
bulblets

Apple Mint
runners

Thyme
stem cuttings

Lemon Balm
runners

Tarragon
root crowns

II.

TREATMENT OF THE HERBS
-PROPAGATION & HARDINESS-
-HARVESTING, DRYING, & STORING-

❦

☾ PROPAGATION

THE ANNUAL herbs are necessarily propagated by seeds, as are also the biennials. Even some perennials are more conveniently increased by seed propagation. Division of clumps, rhizomes, or roots, the use of stem & root cuttings, & the practice of layering are advantageous in individual cases. Vegetative propagation is essential with those herbs, such as tarragon & some of the mints, which rarely, if ever, produce any seeds. Several horticultural varieties of herbs can be maintained only by vegetative means. Some perennials, like fraxinella, which produce seeds abundantly, are best propagated vegetatively, because of the slow seed germination.

The first step in the propagation of herbs is to locate a reliable source of material. Dealers usually handle items for which there is a demand. The Herb Society of America lists names of growers.

Plate 45 shows the various parts used in vegetative propagation. The material was gathered May 1, from plants established for many years in an herb garden at Ithaca, New York; the cuttings could have been made two weeks earlier, before the new growth had advanced to the stage shown.

Information on the propagation of each individual herb is given in the preceding section.

Some perennials, like chives, creeping thyme, & the mints, are most conveniently propagated by division, that is, cutting up the clumps or mats, or the underground parts, & then transplanting. With most plants this is done in spring.

Sage, lavender, lemon verbena, & others may be started from cuttings taken from the growing tips. The pieces should be not more than 3 inches long; at least two nodes should be included. Sand, cinders, vermiculite, & sphagnum are suitable rooting mediums; they should be kept moderately moist, and the cuttings should be protected from draughts. If, as with lemon verbena, cuttings are kept under glass, they should have occasional ventilation. All cuttings should have some shade. Root cuttings are made in fall or winter & are cool-stored in pots of sandy loam before planting out in spring. The mints are propagated from short sections of the stolons.

Layering is a convenient and reliable method. The branches or stems are bent to the ground while still attached to the parent plant and are pegged down carefully to avoid injury. The nodes or joints are then covered with soil. When well rooted, the branches are severed from the old plant. Layering should be done in spring when new growth occurs.

PROPAGATION BY SEEDS

Early seeding indoors has the obvious advantage of providing a much earlier start, enabling the gardener to obtain full use of the entire growing season.

Usually, 6- or 8-inch, shallow flower pots or wooden flats are used. Sandy loam of about one third sand is a good medium. Cinders should be put in the bottom of the pots for drainage. Vermiculite is also a good germinating medium.

Seeds of fraxinella, sweet cicely, & lovage should be sown in late summer, as soon as ripe.

In an established herb garden some plants may self-sow, and the volunteer plants may simply be transplanted to start a new plot. Herbs that self-sow readily are: borage, burnet, caraway, catnip, clary, coriander, dill, German chamomile, horehound, lemon balm, patience, rue, summer savory, winter savory, tansy, & wild marjoram.

Seeds of some herbs germinate promptly under average conditions. These are: basil, borage, burnet, chervil, coriander, cumin, dill, fennel, German chamomile, Roman chamomile, rue, patience, and hyssop.

Herbs noted for the slow or retarded germination of their seeds are: fraxinella, good-king-henry, lavender, lemon balm, Roman wormwood, rosemary, sweet cicely, sweet woodruff, and common wormwood,

Parsley seeds are generally considered to be slow to germinate, but in a test of some freshly gathered seed we obtained good and prompt germination. Some that was put in dry-room storage for two years had 52 per cent. germination.

On page 160 is a table of comparison giving the results of seed germination tests.* The temperature of cold storage in all cases was about 34 to 37 degrees Fahrenheit. The temperature of room storage varied.

⊄ HARDINESS

Most of the biennial & perennial herbs grown in northern gardens are fairly hardy to winter cold. The table on page 161 gives the percentages of plants surviving the winter of 1942-43. For this experiment two herb gardens were maintained, one on clay soil & one on sandy soil; the two gardens were about three miles apart.

*Tests made by M. A. Rice

159

TABLE OF COMPARISON

Name of Plant	Duration of Storage in Months	Percentage of Germination		
		Moist-cold Stored	Dry-cold Stored	Dry-room Stored
Borage	1			60
	24	0	42	52
Burnet	25	18	112	156
seed soaked	0			115
seed not soaked	0			100
Caraway	24	12	14	20
seed soaked	0			5
seed not soaked	0			4
Catnip	24	30	10	14
Chives	24	22	0	0
Coriander	0			30
	20	0	36	83
Dill	24	0	14	30
German Chamomile	24	2	0	0
Good-King-Henry	24	0	0	0
seed soaked	1			3
seed not soaked	1			4
Horehound	24	0	0	8
	0			0
Hyssop	24	0	72	74
Lemon Balm	0			0
	6	7		1
Parsley	24	0	40	52
Patience Dock	24	0	98	100
rough seeds, soaked	0			91
not soaked	0			73
clean seeds, soaked	0			86
not soaked	0			74
Roman Chamomile	24	0	12	20
Rue	24	0	92	94
Summer Savory	23	64	94	92
Thyme	24	0	20	10

The germination period varied from a few days to about a month. In the case of burnet, germination of the soaked seeds continued until the sixty-seventh day. The large percentage of burnet seedlings is due to the fact that some seeds produced two instead of the usual single seedling.

PERCENTAGES OF PLANTS SURVIVING THE WINTER 1942-43, ITHACA, NEW YORK

The mean temperature for Ithaca, December, 1942, was 25°; the mean, January, 1943, was 22°; February, 27°; March, 34°. Lowest temperature was -20° for one day in December; -14° was recorded for several days in February. In the following table, S designates sandy soil, C clay soil. The letter s indicates that 100 per cent. survived; n indicates none survived.

NAME	S	C	NAME	S	C
Allium sativum	s	s	Mentha gentilis	s	s
A. schoenoprasum	s	s	M. piperita	s	s
Anthemis nobilis	80	n	M. pulegium	10	n
Artemisia abrotanum	s	s	M. rotundifolia	s	s
A. absinthium	s	s	M. spicata	s	s
A. dracunculus	70	60	Myrrhis odorata	s	90
A. pontica	s	90	Origanum vulgare	s	60
Asperula odorata	s	20	Petroselinum		
Carum carvi	s	s	crispum	n	n
Chenopodium			Rosmarinus		
bonus-henricus	60	20	officinalis	n	n
Chrysanthemum			Rumex patientia	s	s
balsamita	s	s	Ruta graveolens	s	s
Hyssopus officinalis	s	s	Salvia officinalis	s	90
Lavandula officinalis	s	90		80	n
	n	n	Salvia sclarea	10	n
Levisticum officinale	s	90	Sanguisorba minor	s	s
Majorana hortensis	n	n	Satureja montana	60	50
Marrubium vulgare	70	10	Tanacetum vulgare	s	s
Melissa officinalis	s	s	Thymus serpyllum	s	s
Mentha arvensis	s	s	T. vulgaris	80	n
M. aquatica v. crispa	s	s		s	70

The two sets of percentages for lavender, sage, and thyme indicate that two different genetical strains were tested for hardiness, one being more subject to winter-killing than the other.

ℭ HARVESTING, DRYING, & STORING

Herbs are harvested for their leaves, their seeds or fruits, & their underground parts, such as roots, rhizomes, and bulbs. A good assortment of dried herbs has considerable utility in the home kitchen.

Most herb leaves are preferred fresh and are readily available from the garden through the growing season. Chives, parsley, & many others can be kept growing throughout the winter in a well-lighted room or in a window in the kitchen. Such plants succeed best if they are transplanted in autumn, before they are too big, to pots or to a small box & left outdoors so that they may be subjected to freezing temperatures for about two or three weeks before they are brought indoors.

For harvesting & drying the leaves, most herbs are gathered before flowering. They are cut about mid-morning on a clear, dry day when there is no dew on the plants. Shade-drying is preferable to sun-drying, to retain natural color & minimize the loss of essential oils. Also, for these reasons it is advantageous to hasten the drying by moderate artificial heat, from the kitchen oven perhaps. Fine mesh wire trays are sometimes used, or, without heat, clean paper spread on boards will do.

Some herbs are harvested at full bloom, the entire flowering top being cut, and both leaves and flowers dried, stripped, and pulverized together. Sometimes flowers alone are harvested, as with the chamomiles.

Roots are usually dug in the autumn, & dried whole after washing. Those too large to dry well may be sliced. Artificial heat is advisable, for the roots should be thoroughly dry and brittle before storing.

Shade-drying is preferable for fruits & seeds, although in the production of substantial quantities for market the plants are often mowed and cocked for a time before threshing. Coriander, caraway, anise, & dill seed are field-cured or ripened on canvas sheets or in swaths or cocks. Herbs having fruits or seeds used for flavoring are angelica, anise, burnet, caraway, clary, coriander, cumin, fennel, dill, fenugreek, sweet cicely, and lovage. Most of these require no separation of the seeds from their seed-vessels, except fenugreek, which has pods; the fruits of these herbs are used like seeds, even for planting, and are commonly called seeds.

In harvesting the seeds, it is best to gather them in the early stages of ripening, first, to avoid unnecessary losses from shattering, second, to obtain a

162

bright, clean, & attractive product, and third, to conserve the essential oils. Seeds harvested for culinary purposes may also be used for planting, provided that viability has not been impaired by too long storage or other treatment.

Dried herb materials are most conveniently used in powdered form. Leaves and flowers are stripped from their stalks and hand-rubbed until pulverized. The coarser parts are sifted out and discarded. Seeds or fruits are powdered by some method of grinding. An old-fashioned, kitchen coffee grinder may be used, if obtainable. There are also small, hand flour-mills; the motor-driven ones are rather expensive. Seeds may also be pulverized by pounding in an iron or stone mortar. Even a flat-iron might be used for a crusher. Dust resulting from handling dried herbs may induce a temporary hay-fever in susceptible individuals. Discomfort may be largely avoided by tying a moist cloth over the nose and mouth. If much processing of dried herbs is done, a standard dust-mask should be obtained.

For storage, glass screw-capped jars are most convenient. They should be as nearly air-tight as possible. Corks are also used. If jars of brown or other colored glass are available, they are preferable, since the herb material must be kept away from light to retain color. Jars may also be kept in closed or curtained shelves or in a dark room. The herb material must be entirely dry, for the presence of even a little moisture in the jar may cause molds & ruin the contents. If condensation appears inside the glass, the jar should be opened and the contents allowed to dry out. Herbs are sometimes stored in paper bags; these exclude dust & insects, but also permit the rapid loss of volatile oils. In the country, herbs are often simply cut, tied in bunches, & hung up on the walls or from the rafters in the kitchen, attic, or barn. This is poor practice, since the flavors are dissipated, dust and grime settle on the material, insects have free access, & much material is scattered on the floor and lost.

Herb teas or tisanes are made by pouring boiling water on the herb & allowing it to steep for a few minutes. A teaspoonful of herb is used to each cup of water. Decoction, or active boiling, is the procedure with lemon verbena, Roman wormwood and common wormwood, horehound, hyssop, bergamot, bee balm, sweet woodruff, lemon balm, and flowers of lavender. Herbs may be blended. Sugar or honey are added. Milk is usually put only into catnip and chamomile infusions.

Following are a few words on harvesting and drying various kinds of herbs. Section I gives directions for others.

163

Anise. Seeds are collected by pulling up the plants entirely or by cutting them. This must be done when the seed-tips become gray-green to avoid darkening of the seeds by weather exposure. The plants are then spread out to dry and are later threshed. Flowers are occasionally dried & powdered for flavoring, especially in wine.

Basil. The stems are cut off close to the ground about the time blooming begins and are treated like mint. New growth from the stumps provides one or two additional crops before the end of the growing season.

Bee Balm. Treatment is about the same as for mint.

Chervil. Fresh leaves are harvested and used like parsley. Seeds for flavoring vinegar or for planting are stripped off by hand, dried, winnowed if necessary, & stored.

Clary. Flowers for infusions are gathered by cutting off the stalks at the height of bloom, drying, & separating later. Collecting the seeds is difficult, for they shatter quickly when ripe and also ripen irregularly during a long period; see the method for borage, page 78.

Coriander. Fruits are collected as soon as full-sized. Tops are cut & laid out to dry for shaking & winnowing.

Costmary is handled similarly to mint.

Cumin is handled much like caraway.

Fennel. Foliage is simply cut off, dried, & crumbled in the usual way. Seeds are harvested like dill.

Fenugreek. Fruits are picked as soon as ripe but before the seeds shatter. Seeds are shelled or threshed from the pods and dried by artificial heat.

Horehound. The upper parts are cut just before flowering and are handled like mint. Soil is apt to cling to the rough foliage, which should probably be washed prior to drying.

Lemon Balm is handled similarly to mint.

Lemon Verbena. Leaves are picked singly for drying and pulverizing.

Lovage. Fruits are handled about like caraway. Leaves are picked while young, thin, and tender, older ones being tough and usually damaged by insects and disease. Roots are dug in late autumn of the second year, washed, sliced crosswise, and dried by artificial heat at about 125 degrees Fahrenheit.

Mint. Shoots are cut just before blooming, on a dry day, and are shade-dried. The material is spread out or hung up in bunches; when thoroughly dry, it is stripped & pulverized.

Parsley. Foliage is handled like mint. To obtain a supply of seed, the umbels are cut at maturity, when the fruits turn brown. They are laid out on sheets & the fruits beaten off with a stick or flail. Several beatings are necessary for maximum harvest. The roots are

164

occasionally dried; they are dug in late fall of the second year.

Roman Wormwood is handled like mint. Plants may also be harvested when in bloom, to include flowers as part of the dried product.

Rue is used mostly fresh, but may be dried like other herbs.

Sage. The tender, herbaceous parts are cut and handled like mint. Only one cutting should be made the first year, toward the end of the season, but two or three may be made in each of the following years, depending on the growth. Plants become more woody with age, and are usually grubbed out in their fourth to sixth year. A few new plants should be set out each year to keep a succession going.

Southernwood is treated like mint.

Summer Savory. The whole plant is cut at ground level at the beginning of bloom. It is dried like mint.

Sweet Cicely is handled like caraway.

Sweet Marjoram is used mostly in fresh condition & is often grown indoors in winter. It is also dried.

Tansy is cut at full bloom. Leaves & flowers are crumbled separately or as a mixture.

Thyme. Blooming tops with some foliage are cut, blossoms forming part of the powdered product. This is sifted to discard coarse stem material. Two or three crops may be cut in a season.

Wild Marjoram is handled like mint.

Winter Savory. Cutting stimulates new growth. Two crops may be had, midseason & late.

PLATE 46

Two thirds
natural size

Urtica dioica

III.
WILD POT-HERBS
THEIR DESCRIPTIONS & USE

🌿

A GREAT many wild plants are edible, but only a few really taste good. These are the ones included in this book. Several are common weeds and are readily found near dwellings.

Plants are generally not well-flavored at an advanced stage of development. Near flowering time they are apt to become tough & bitter. New spring growth is best. Most of the illustrations show the plants at the proper stage for gathering.

The ranges of distribution given for the various plants are the approximate areas in which they are known to be very common. Their complete ranges may be much greater. Eleven native plants of North America and seven introduced plants are included. A few are both native & introduced.

167

CURTICACEAE · NETTLE FAMILY

THE PLANTS may be herbaceous or woody. The leaves are simple, stipulate, & often have stinging hairs. The flowers are in spikes or clusters.

Species of URTICA · NETTLES

French: Ortie. German: Brennessel. Italian: Ortica.

THE stinging nettle, *Urtica dioica* L., also called tall nettle, is a perennial, reproducing by seeds and creeping rootstocks. The ridged stems reach a height of 2 or 3 feet & are covered with stinging hairs. The leaves are opposite, ovate to heart-shaped, coarsely serrate, hairy, & rather long-petioled; the stipules are distinct. The flowers, mostly dioecious, are small and green, in branching, panicled spikes.

Widespread but infrequent throughout the eastern United States, the plant is found blooming from July to September in neglected yards, dumps, waste places, & along roadsides, in rich soil. It was introduced from Eurasia. See Plate 46.

Similar to the preceding species, & likewise a perennial, *U. gracilis* Ait. differs in being more slender, less hairy, & has narrow, nearly smooth leaves with finely serrate margins; the flowers are monoecious.

Native in North America, *U. gracilis* is widely distributed in the northern United States & southern Canada, where it is found in barnyards & neglected fields in rich, damp loam. It flowers during

July and August.

U. urens L., called small nettle, is an annual. The stems are branched from the base, somewhat hairy, 4 to 24 inches high. The flowers, growing in axillary clusters, are dioecious.

Well-distributed but rare in the eastern United States, common on the Pacific Coast, the small nettle is found blooming from May to August in neglected gardens, fields, and orchards. It came from Europe.

Other species are *U. procera* Muhl., native and common in the eastern United States and Canada, *U. lyallii* Wats. & *U. holosericea* Nutt., the two last named being native western species.

Nettles are cooked like spinach. Very little water is needed for stewing them. Salt, pepper, and butter or margarine are added after cooking, & hard-boiled eggs may be used as garnish. The stinging principle is dissipated by cooking. The Scotch dish, nettle pudding, is made of nettles, leeks, cabbage, & rice boiled together; soup may also be made from nettles. The stem-fibers have been used in parts of Europe and the British Isles for making cloth and paper. Roots and leaves have been used for dyeing. The nettle is antiscorbutic, but its reputed medicinal properties are probably weak.

PLATE 47

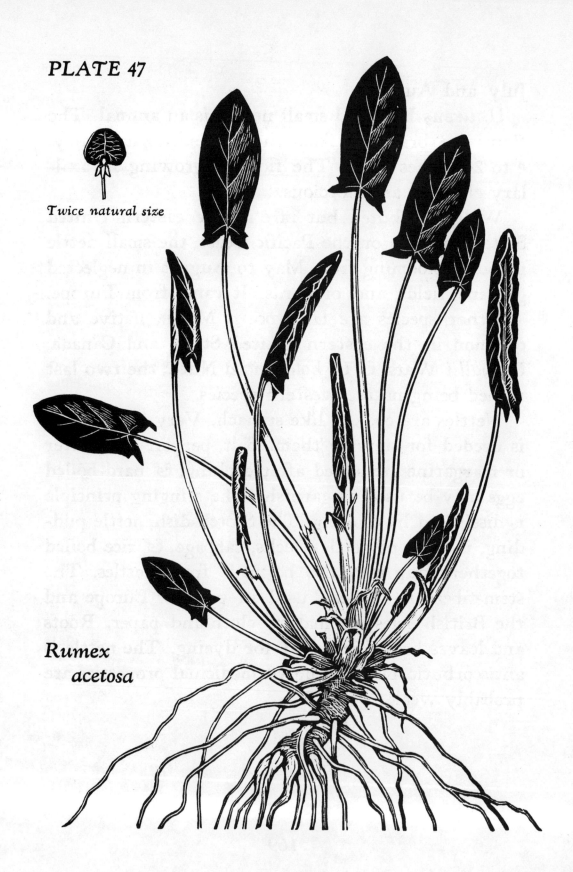

Twice natural size

Rumex
acetosa

❡ POLYGONACEAE ‧ BUCKWHEAT FAMILY

See page 21 for a description of this family.

❧

RUMEX ACETOSA ‧ SOUR DOCK

Also called Garden Sorrel, English Sorrel,
Green Sauce, Sour Dabs, Sour Suds, Cuckoo Sorrow.
French: Oseille sauvage, Vinette, Surelle.
German: Grosser Sauerampfer. Italian: Acetosa.

SOUR DOCK is a perennial, reproducing by seeds
and creeping roots. The stems are erect & slender,
sometimes scattered, often in clumps, the basal leaves
simple, entire, oblong to broadly lanceolate, saggitate
at the base, glabrous. The largest leaves may reach
a length of 6 inches. The stem-leaves are smaller,
nearly sessile, arrow-shaped & undulate; stipules are
present and form a sheath. The small green flowers
are in terminal panicles.* Plate 47 shows young plants.

In garden culture sour dock is propagated by seeds
and by root division; it tends to self-sow. The plants
are adapted to rich, moist garden soil and full sun.
They are spaced about a foot apart in the row.

Like R. *patientia,* sour dock is often attacked by
a black aphis, which causes the leaves to curl; the
plant is also subject to a shot-hole fungus disease of
the leaves. Both aphis and fungus disease are most
evident in mid-season or later and are absent from

*See the note on page 174.

171

the new leaves of spring growth. The leaves of sour dock sometimes cause a dermatitis when handled by susceptible persons.

Usually only the early spring growth is used as a pot-herb, although the flavor at that stage is considered too mild by some people. In cultivation, new growth may be induced by cutting back the plants before they bloom. Several crops may be had in one season, but the later ones are much more acid. To cook sour dock, wash the fresh leaves in cold water, then put them in a pan of fresh water & heat until just below boiling; if boiled, they become too soft. Rinse & drain them in a colander. Make a sauce of melted butter, flour, milk or cream, & an egg-yolk. Season the sauce with salt & nutmeg, add the dock leaves, & let the mixture come to a boil. The dish is then ready to serve & may be covered with strips of bread browned in butter. It goes well with liver, cutlets, boiled ham, or lamb. Cream soups may be thickened with dock leaves, and the leaves are also added to salads or cooked with other greens.

The plant is strongly antiscorbutic. Its reputed medicinal properties are probably weak.

Native in Europe & Asia, the plant has become naturalized in America, where it is found wild from Vermont to Pennsylvania. Infrequent except in the North Atlantic states where it is locally abundant, sour dock is found in waste places, old pastures and moist permanent meadows.

PLATE 48

Five times
natural size

Rumex acetosella

RUMEX ACETOSELLA L. - SHEEP SORREL

Also called Field Sorrel, Horse Sorrel, Sour Grass,
Red-top Sorrel, Mountain Sorrel, Red Weed.
French: Petite Oseille, Vinette sauvage.
German: Kleiner Sauerampfer. Italian: Acetosella.

A PERENNIAL, sheep sorrel reproduces by seeds
and creeping roots. The stems reach a height of 12
inches and are usually scattered along the creeping
root system. The leaves are alternate, simple, entire,
from halberd-shaped at the base of the plant to nar-
rowly lanceolate or linear at the upper part of the
stem. The minute flowers, which ultimately turn
red in color, are in terminal panicles.*

Culinary use is similar to that of sour dock.

Introduced from Eurasia, sheep sorrel is a common
weed throughout the United States. Its habitat is
sandy or gravelly fields & meadows with dry, sterile
soil. Flowering time is from May to September.

Young growth is shown in Plate 48.

*Unlike those of other species, the dried calyx-valves do
not exceed the achene but closely cover it. The achene is
triangular, reddish-brown, glossy. In R. *acetosa* the calyx-
valves are enlarged, broadly rounded, the base cordate and
with a tubercle. The achene is dark brown. The fruits of
these two species are shown enlarged in Plates 47 and 48.

174

ℭ CHENOPODIACEAE · GOOSEFOOT FAMILY

This family is described on page 25.

❦

CHENOPODIUM ALBUM L. · PIGWEED

Also called Lamb's Quarters, White Goosefoot,
Fat Hen, Mealweed, Frost-blite & Bacon-weed.
French: Ansérine blanche, Farineuse.
German: Weisser Gänsefuss.

THE PLANT is annual. It has smooth, angular, striate stems, branching above, the height ranging from 20 inches to more than 6 feet. The leaves are alternate, simple, rhombic to lanceolate, mealy especially on the underside, margins broadly and sparsely toothed. The small, green flowers are in irregular spikes clustered in panicles. The lens-shaped seeds are black & glossy, the papery pericarp usually adhering to them. A young plant is shown in Plate 49.

For eating raw or for cooking, only plants under 8 inches high should be used. The leaves are cooked like spinach, and the ripe seeds may be dried and cooked like oatmeal.

Pigweed is a common weed throughout the United States, blooming from June to September in gardens, grain fields, and other cultivated land, and also on waste ground. It was introduced from Eurasia.

PLATE 49

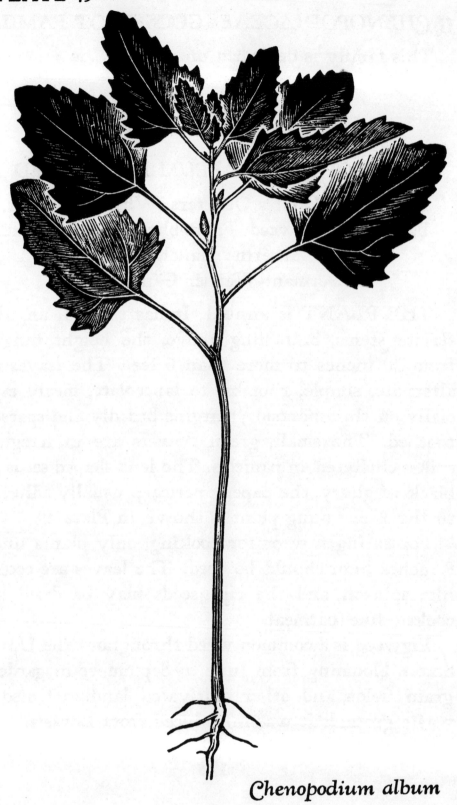

Chenopodium album

ℂ PHYTOLACCACEAE ⸱ POKEWEED FAMILY

A SMALL family, the *Phytolaccaceae* are characterized by apetalous, perfect flowers, usually with many carpels in a ring; the flowers are usually in a raceme. Leaves are alternate and entire. Some members of the family are trees or shrubs; even the herbaceous ones tend to be woody at the base. The fruit is a berry.

PHYTOLACCA AMERICANA L. ⸱ POKEWEED

Also called Pokeberry, Scoke, Pigeon Berry, Garget, Inkberry, Red-ink Plant, Coakum, Cancer Jalap. French: Raisin d'Amérique. German: Kermesbeere. Italian: Fitolacca, Erba cremesina.

POKEWEED is perennial, reproducing by seeds. The stout, smooth, hollow stems rise from a large, fleshy, white root, are usually branched above, and reach a height of 6 to 9 feet. The leaves are ovate, alternate, simple, entire, and long-petioled. Flowers are small & white, with five, broad, petal-like sepals; they are borne in elongate, terminal racemes. There are ten stamens & ten united carpels. The fruit is a purple berry with red juice. Early top growth and a single flower are shown on page 178.

Fruits of the pokeweed are inedible & the root is

*Five times
natural size*

poisonous. Only new spring growth under 5 inches should be used for eating; the leaves should be boiled and the first water discarded. They should then be cooked thoroughly in an uncovered pot and served like spinach, with butter & salt, or with vinegar or white sauce.

Native in North America, pokeweed is locally frequent from Maine to Minnesota & southward, and is found in pasture lands & woodlands in rich gravelly soil. It blooms through July and August. Introduced into Europe as an ornamental, pokeweed was also once used in southern Europe for coloring wine.

ℂ PORTULACACEAE · PURSLANE FAMILY

MEMBERS of the family are low, succulent plants with simple, entire leaves. The flowers open only in sunshine & last but a short time. Petals, when present, are five in number; there are two sepals.

PORTULACA OLERACEA L. - PURSLANE

Also called Pussley, Pursley.
French: Pourpier potager. German: Gelber Portulak.
Italian: Porcellana, Sportellacchia.

A LOW, mat-forming annual, purslane is much branched, the stems smooth, succulent, & often red in color. The leaves are alternate or clustered, succulent, simple, entire, obovate or wedge-shaped. The flowers are small, axillary, & sessile. The buds are pointed, their yellow petals opening only in the sun.

The plant is juicy & good to eat either cooked or raw. The following method of preparing it is highly esteemed in Europe: first wash & drain the leaves. Melt a piece of butter, stir some zwieback crumbs into it until the mixture turns uniformly yellow, then add the leaves & let the whole simmer on the burner. Meanwhile stir in sufficient meat broth to form a sauce. Lastly stir in some rich cream or the yolk of an egg.

Widespread and locally common throughout the

179

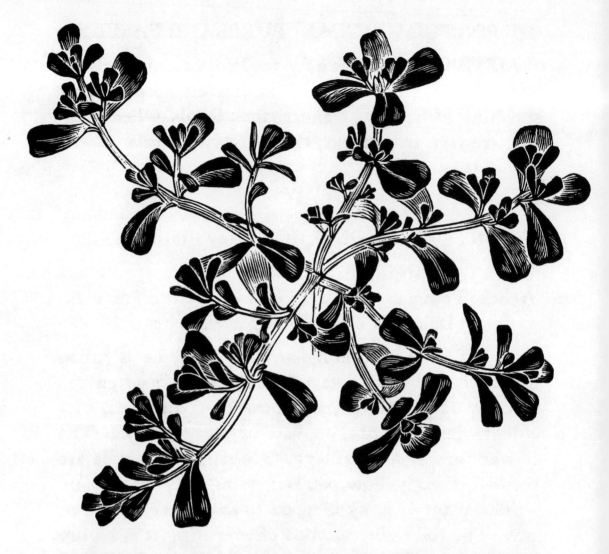

United States & southern Canada, purslane is found as a weed in waste places, gardens, and cultivated fields, usually in rich soil. Flowering time is from June to September. The plant is a native of Europe and is widely distributed in most temperate regions of the world. It is able to withstand a considerable degree of dryness.

A plant is illustrated above.

ℂ RANUNCULACEAE ⸱ CROWFOOT FAMILY

MOST OF the plants of this family are herbaceous. Many have dissected leaves. The flowers are sometimes apetalous, the calyx resembling a corolla. All floral parts are distinct, that is, not fused or attached to one another. The stamens are numerous in most cases. A large family, the *Ranunculaceae* contain many familiar wild and cultivated plants, such as the buttercup, hepatica, columbine, aconite, peony, delphinium, and clematis.

CALTHA PALUSTRIS L. ⸱ COWSLIP

Also called Marsh Marigold & Kingcup.
French: Pacoteure, Populage, Souci d'eau.
German: Sumpf-Dotterblume. Italian: Farferugine.

THE COWSLIP is a low, perennial plant, 8 to 24 inches high, with smooth, hollow, ridged stems that rise from a stout, creeping rootstock. The smooth, dark green leaves are round to kidney-shaped with crenate margins, the basal leaves petioled, the upper sessile. The flowers have no petals, but the broad, deep yellow, petal-like sepals are conspicuous.

For eating, only the leaves that appear before the blooming period should be used; the best stage is as shown in Plate 50. New growth may be gathered several times before flowering. The leaves are boiled

PLATE 50

Caltha palustris

like spinach & are served with sauce, butter or margarine, or eggs. They may be used raw in salads.

The cowslip is found blooming in April & May in wet woods, wet meadows, swamps and bogs. Introduced from Eurasia, it grows in North America from Newfoundland to Alaska & southward to Tennessee and Nebraska.

❧

⁅ CRUCIFERAE ⸱ MUSTARD FAMILY

See page 29 for a description of this family.

BARBAREA VULGARIS R. Br.

Winter Cress, Mountain Cress, St. Barbara's Cress, Bitter Cress, Yellow Rocket, Yellow-weed, Pot-herb. French: Herbe de Ste. Barbe. German: Barbenkraut.

A PERENNIAL or biennial, winter cress reproduces by seeds or by new shoots from old roots. The stems, often clustered, are erect, grooved, & smooth. The basal leaves have a broad terminal lobe & sometimes as many as four small lateral lobes; they are dark green, smooth, glossy, and somewhat succulent. The flowers are yellow and are borne in racemes. The seed-pods are long & more or less erect on thin pedicels. The rosettes of new leaves which appear in spring & late fall are conspicuous and characteristic;

183

one is shown on this page; they are the parts used
for culinary purposes.

For salad they are used with the usual dressings;
they may be chopped & sprinkled over potatoes or
used as garnish for fish dishes. As a pot-herb cooked
like spinach, winter cress tends to be too bitter for
some tastes & may be mixed with other greens.

A common weed in the northeastern and north
central states, the plant occurs less frequently west-

ward. It is native in northern North America but was also introduced from Eurasia. It is found on cultivated lands, newly seeded lawns, & new meadows, on rich soil. Flowering time is from May to June.

Barbarea verna, known as spring cress or scurvy grass, is a garden plant brought in from Europe and somewhat naturalized in the east. It resembles winter cress, but usually has more than four lobes on each side of the leaf, & the pedicels are more nearly equal to the pods in thickness.

❦

BRASSICA KABER (D. C.) L. Wheeler

Called Field Mustard, Field Kale, Charlock, Kedlock.
French: Moutarde des Champs, Jotte, Raveluche.
German: Wilder Senf, Bruchhederich.
Italian: Senapa selvatica, Senapino, Rapaccini.

AN ANNUAL reproducing by seeds, field mustard has erect, bristly stems 1 to 2 feet high, the upper portion branched & somewhat spreading. The lower leaves are alternate, petioled, hairy, and pinnately divided into a broad terminal lobe & smaller lateral lobes; the upper leaves are oblong to ovate, acute, sessile, dentate, & hairy. The conspicuous yellow flowers are in racemes. A plant at the best stage for use is shown in Plate 51.*

The leaves are cooked like spinach & served with

*See Plate 56 for other edible mustards.

185

PLATE 51

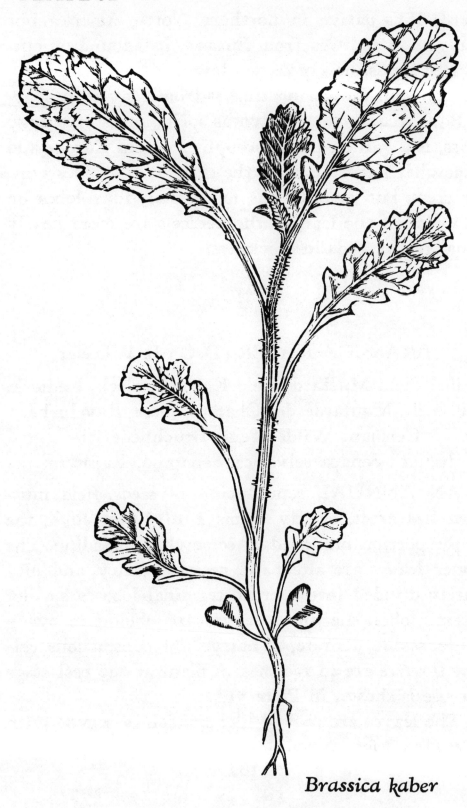

Brassica kaber

egg dishes or meats; they may also be mixed with other pot-herbs to add a peppery flavor.

Introduced from Eurasia, field mustard has become a weed throughout the grain sections of the United States, but it is most frequent in the northeast, particularly in oat fields. It is also found on other cultivated & waste land. It starts to bloom in June.

༃

NASTURTIUM OFFICINALE R. Br.
WATER CRESS

French: Cresson, Crinson. German: Brunnenkresse. Italian: Cressione di sorgenti, Nasturzio aquatico.

AN AQUATIC perennial, water cress normally grows in cold, spring-fed brooks & ponds, where it sometimes forms floating mats on the water. It has branching, creeping, angular stems turning up at the tips & rooting freely at the nodes. Leaves are alternate, pinnately divided, the leaflets three to eleven in number, round or elliptical, & nearly entire. The small white flowers are on slender pedicels and are borne in racemes. The seed-pods are linear, sometimes more than an inch long, short-beaked. See Plate 52.

The terminal sprigs are used as a garnish and for salad, either alone or combined with other greens. They may be used as sandwich filling or as a pungent relish with various meat, fish, egg, and cheese

PLATE 52

Nasturtium officinale

dishes. Chopped leaves are incorporated in fruit and vegetable juice cocktails, in soups, and in biscuits. Water cress is a valuable source of ascorbic acid or vitamin C and is also a stimulant to the appetite and the digestive processes.

The plant is propagated by seeds & more often by stem cuttings from the tips. It thrives in clear, cool, preferably moving water & is especially favored by the presence of lime and a substratum of rich compost. Winter-killing may be averted by increased flooding and temporary submergence during freezing weather. Water cress may be forced in winter if it is grown in a cool greenhouse in rich, continually moist, calcareous soil, under partial shade. It is grown commercially in parts of the South, the industry being dependent on the warm limestone springs of the districts. Plants are also gathered in the wild for local markets.

Native in Europe and the temperate zone of Asia, water cress is now naturalized throughout a large part of the United States & southern Canada, living over winter in the vegetative condition in protected habitats where it is not subjected to hard freezing.

LEPIDIUM VIRGINICUM L. - PEPPERGRASS

Poor-man's-pepper, Bird's Pepper, Tongue-grass.

AN ANNUAL or biennial, peppergrass has erect, stiff, nearly smooth stems, branched above, reaching 8 to 30 inches in height. The leaves are alternate, the basal ones pinnately lobed or toothed, those of the stem becoming successively narrower and more nearly entire toward the top of the plant. The small white or greenish flowers are on slender pedicels; two stamens are present; the flowers are in racemes. The fruits are nearly orbicular, somewhat narrower at the base, notched at the top; a small plant in fruit is shown in Plate 53.

The leaves are best as a garnish or in salad, but they are also cooked as a pot-herb.

A native American plant, *L. virginicum* is widespread from the Atlantic Coast to the Rocky Mountains. It is found in grain fields, new seedings, and other cultivated ground, also in waste places, in dry soil. It blooms from May to October.

L. sativum L. is a cultivated species introduced from Europe & somewhat escaped. It is known as garden cress and is similar to *L. virginicum* in general appearance, but the plant is glaucous. It has six stamens, stout pedicels, and the fruits are ovate.

⟨ ASCLEPIADACEAE · MILKWEED FAMILY

THE PLANTS have entire, mostly opposite leaves and five-parted flowers. A typical flower is described below. Most members of the family are tropical. Several of them yield useful fibers. All have a milky juice which has emetic & purgative properties.

ASCLEPIAS SYRIACA L. - MILKWEED

Also called Silkweed & Cottonweed.
French: Herbe à ouate. German: Seidenpflanze.

COMMON milkweed is a stout perennial with erect, pubescent, mostly unbranched stems 2 to 5 feet high. Plants usually grow in clumps from the long creeping rootstocks. Leaves are opposite or whorled, simple, entire, broadly oval to oblong-elliptic, smooth above & downy beneath, 4 to 8 inches long, short-petioled, the veins uniting before reaching the margin. The corolla is five-parted, reflexed, pinkish to purplish. A crown is present, and consists of five hooded bodies, an incurved horn rising from the cavity of each hood. The filaments of the stamens are united in a tube surrounding the pistil. The anthers are adherent to the stigma. The inflorescence is a many-flowered umbel. The hairy, pod-like fruit is covered with soft spine-like projections. The seeds are flat, dull brown, & bear a tuft of long silky hair.

191

PLATE 53

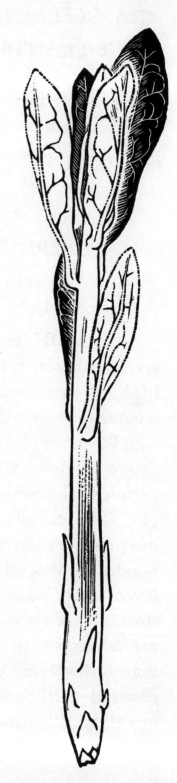

Lepidium virginicum   *Asclepias syriaca*

For cooking, none but the early summer shoots under 8 inches high should be used. They are cooked like asparagus, which some say they surpass in flavor, & may be served on toast with sauce, or plain with melted butter. The young flower buds may be cooked as greens. Plants should not be eaten raw or at an advanced stage. The proper size for gathering is shown in Plate 53.

Milkweed is found in fields, pastures, and waste places, in rich gravelly loam. It is native & common in eastern North America. It flowers from June to August. The plant was introduced into Europe as an ornamental in the seventeenth century. At the time of Frederick the Great, milkweed was grown extensively in Prussia for the textile industry.

⟨ HYDROPHYLLACEAE
WATERLEAF FAMILY

ALTHOUGH cosmopolitan in its distribution, this small family is best represented in North America. The plants are mostly herbaceous, the flowers solitary or more often in one-sided cymes or apparent racemes coiled when in bud. The flowers are five-parted, regular & perfect, the calyx deeply notched, the petals united. The five stamens are borne on the corolla, alternate with its lobes.

PLATE 54

Hydrophyllum virginianum

HYDROPHYLLUM VIRGINIANUM L.

Called Waterleaf, Indian Salad, Shawnee Salad,
John's Cabbage, & Brook Flower.

A PERENNIAL plant rising from scaly rhizomes, waterleaf may reach a height of 3 feet; it tends to sprawl. The leaves are alternate, pinnately divided into as many as seven cut-toothed segments, and are often gray-spotted or blotched on the upper surface when young. The spots give the appearance of drops of water clinging to the leaves, which perhaps explains the common name. The flowers are white to purple, in peduncled cymes, the peduncles often confluent with the petioles for part of their length. The calyx-lobes are long, narrow, & ciliate; the lobes of the corolla are erect, the stamens exserted. Plate 54 shows a young plant at the best stage for gathering.

Waterleaf was an esculent plant of the American Indians. Its flavor is bland and agreeable, becoming stronger with age; the plant is probably rich in vitamins and is a good antiscorbutic. The tender young stems & leaves are cooked like spinach or are eaten raw out of hand or in salads.

The plant is found in rich woods; it blooms from May to August. Favored by shade, it is sometimes cultivated as an ornamental border or in foundation plantings on the north side of buildings. It is propagated by seeds.

Waterleaf is indigenous in North America.

195

PLATE 55

Cichorium intybus

ℭ COMPOSITAE · COMPOSITE FAMILY

See the description on page 139.

CICHORIUM INTYBUS L. · CHICORY

Also called Succory, Coffeeweed, Blue Sailors, Bunk.
When grown in compact heads for winter salad,
called Witloof Chicory & French Endive.
Small blanched leaves grown in darkness called
Barbe de capucin. French: Chicorée sauvage,
Barbe de capucin. German: Zichorie, Sonnenwedel.
Italian: Cicoria selvatica, Radicchio.

A PERENNIAL with a long tap-root, chicory has stiff, erect stems, much branched, hollow, pubescent, with milky juice; they grow from 2 to 6 feet high. The basal leaves are dentate, runcinate-pinnatifid, sometimes reaching 8 inches in length; the upper are alternate, clasping, hairy, oblong-lanceolate, entire to dentate, auriculate. The flower-heads are axillary, sessile, two to three in a cluster, or solitary on short branches. The bright blue flowers are all ligulate. Plate 55 shows a young plant and the top of an inflorescence. There are several cultivated field varieties grown for their enlarged roots. Garden & truck varieties are grown principally for greens.

The young tender leaves are eaten raw in salads and are also served like spinach, after boiling in two waters. The roots also may be boiled as a vegetable. Chicory is used principally to flavor or adulterate coffee. The enlarged roots of cultivated varieties are dried, roasted with fat, & ground; the roasted root contains inulin, dextrose, levulose, & caramel, & it imparts body, dark coloring, and special flavoring to coffee. The amount of ground root used varies from one ounce in a pound of coffee to as much as one part of root to three parts of coffee. Medicinal properties of chicory are weak.

In garden culture, propagation is by seeds sown in late spring in rows 15 to 24 inches apart. Seedlings are thinned to stand 4 to 8 inches apart in the rows. The young leaves are used the following spring. The plants are sometimes blanched by banking with soil. For winter salad, Witloof roots are dug the first fall and stored in a cold place. Tops, side roots, and root-tips should be trimmed off. After several days the roots are brought in to a temperature of 50 or 60 degrees and covered with several inches of earth, sand, or sawdust. They are kept slightly moist. The shoots are ready in about four weeks. For Barbe de capucin, the roots are forced in a warm dark place, but are not covered with earth. Wild chicory may be used as Barbe de capucin.

Native in Europe, chicory is an introduced weed in the United States. It is especially prevalent in the northeastern states, in old hayfields & waste places. Root varieties are cultivated extensively in Belgium.

TARAXACUM OFFICINALE Weber

Dandelion, Lion's Tooth, Blow-ball, Cankerwort.
French: Dent de lion, Coq.
German: Kuhblume, Löwenzahn.
Italian: Dente di leone, Capo di frate, Tarassaco.

THIS familiar weed is a perennial with a thick, long tap-root & a very short stem, bearing a rosette of leaves & several smooth, hollow scapes; the juice is milky. The leaves are oblong to spatulate, & vary from nearly entire to runcinate-pinnatifid; they may reach a length of 12 inches. The solitary heads are composed of golden-yellow, ligulate florets; the outer row of involucral bracts is reflexed. The achene is spindle-shaped, terminating in a long beak bearing a white pappus, the entire mass of pappus forming a fluffy ball. Selected leaf-forms are sometimes cultivated in herb & vegetable gardens.

Tender young leaves may be eaten raw in salads or cooked like spinach; the sliced root is also added to salads or pot-herbs. Leaves are usable throughout the summer & are often canned. Wine is sometimes made from the leaves and flowers. The dried roots constitute a crude drug called taraxacum, and when roasted & ground, are used as a coffee substitute or mixture. The drug probably does not have therapeutic value, but the green parts of the dandelion are antiscorbutic.

Dandelion is found in lawns, meadows, and pas-

199

tures. It was introduced from Eurasia and according
to some authorities is also native in North America.

In the culture of garden varieties, seeds are sown
in spring in rows 18 inches apart, and the seedlings
are later thinned to stand 15 to 18 inches apart. The
leaves may be bleached by tying them together and
covering them with soil. Roots may be forced for
winter salad by digging them in fall & storing like
Witloof chicory or French endive. Roots to be used
for drug or beverage purposes are dug in the fall of
the second year, washed, & dried whole or in short
pieces or slices. Dandelion is extremely hardy and
adaptable but is favored by sandy loam soils.

IV.

THE CLASSIFICATION
AND
NAMING OF PLANTS

FEW AMATEUR plant enthusiasts appreciate the value and significance of the scientific names of plants, & few are familiar with the systematic subdivision of the vegetable kingdom into smaller related groups for purposes of scientific research. The following brief attempt at an explanation may help to answer some of the questions puzzling gardeners, growers, & purchasers of herb plants and materials.

The many different kinds of plants that exist throughout the world constitute what is called the vegetable kingdom. According to some authorities there are more than 200,000 different *species* or kinds of plants. For convenience in studying the members of this vast body, the kingdom is subdivided into smaller groups which are based on natural relationships. The principal groups or classifications mentioned in this book are *species*, *genera* (singular *genus*), & *families*.

Some members of the plant kingdom are more closely related by characteristics which they have in common. Plants that differ only slightly from one another are said to belong to the same species. For example, although no two individual plants of *Nepeta cataria* are identical, all of them are sufficiently alike to be recognized as the same species.

Two or more kinds of plants not sufficiently alike to be of the same species, but related by important characteristics that they have in common, are grouped into a genus. For example,

Mentha citrata, M. arvensis, & M. piperita are different kinds of plants, but all of them are mints & form part of the genus *Mentha*. Genera considered to be related constitute a *family*, as, for example, *Mentha, Nepeta, Monarda, &* other related genera make up the *Labiatae*. They differ distinctly from one another but are held together by certain characteristics common to all of them.

It is essential that each kind of plant should have a name which distinguishes it from all other kinds and which applies to that particular kind alone. Since there is no scientific basis for common or colloquial names, they come into use fortuitously and are frequently numerous & confusing; a plant may be known by different names in different localities, or several plants may be designated by the same name; a plant is known by a different name in every country, the name being understood generally only by persons familiar with the language of the particular region. In order to eliminate ambiguity and to establish a name for each plant that will be the same in all parts of the world, botanists have chosen Latin as the language for describing and naming plants. Greek words are also sometimes used in plant names. In writing a name, the name of the genus is placed first; this is followed by the specific (*species*) name. In botanical literature, this is followed by the name, usually abbreviated, of the person who first named the plant. Many of the plant names in this book are followed by an L., which stands for Carl Linnaeus, the famous eighteenth century Swedish naturalist who described and named a great many plants.

Home gardeners are often confused by the changes in scientific names which they sometimes find in catalogs and other publications. These changes are understandable to the reader when he becomes aware that trained botanists throughout the world are constantly studying plants, uncovering new facts about them, and adjusting earlier inaccuracies of observation. If, after thorough investigation, a botanist decides that a plant has been incorrectly named, he may publish another name for it, setting forth his reasons for doing so. These are usually published in the form of an article in a scientific magazine. Following this section is a list of the synonyms that the reader may find in herb books or catalogs.

A word should be said about variation in plants. As stated on the preceding page, plants of the same species differ only slightly from one another, but some species show a greater latitude of deviation than others, such as creeping thyme, for example. Variation is sometimes the result of *hybridization*, the breeding of two different species or forms of a species. The mints hybridize readily, & this tendency to cross freely gives rise to so many different forms that the identification of the mints often becomes a problem for specialists. The offspring of such a cross is called a *hybrid*. The seeds of hybrid varieties may have low viability or may not produce plants like the parent; such varieties are propagated vegetatively.

Variation is also a result of environment. Climate, weather conditions, soil, and light all play their part in affecting the growth & forms of plants. In the case of herbs, where flavor is so important, growers should consider environmental factors as they affect the essential oils and other substances in plants. Sweet woodruff is a striking case of variation in flavor brought about by climatic conditions or other factors. The woodruff of Europe is the same botanical species as the plant grown in this country, but connoisseurs generally agree that the flavors do not compare. The same is true of the controversial herb, origano, which, because of its tendency to vary in flavor & appearance, is almost a different herb to each person who uses it.

Variations due to environment are independent of the genetical inheritance of a species & are not constant or entirely predictable. It seems of doubtful value to honor unstable, environmental forms with individual names. The amateur horticulturist assumes that there must be a name for every new variation and is often misled by the variety names listed in catalogs. Such names are frequently employed by commercial growers before the plants have been thoroughly studied to determine their botanical status. The subject of varieties requires thorough investigation by botanical specialists. it is not an exaggeration to state that one man may spend a lifetime on the study of a single genus. The study of plants is a living process, its results constantly modified by further knowledge.

———————

In the following list of synonyms, the first name in each group is the one used in this book.

SYNONYMS

(*indicates currently preferred name as listed in *Hortus Third: A Concise Diction-ary of Plants Cultivated in the United States and Canada,* initially compiled by Liberty Hyde Bailey and Ethel Zoe Bailey, revised and expanded by the staff of the Liberty Hyde Bailey Hortorium, Cornell University, 1976.)

Agastache foeniculum (Pursh) Ktze.*
  A. anethiodora Britt.
Allium ascalonicum L.
  A. cepa L. Aggregatum Group*
Allium cepa v. viviparum Metz
  A. cepa v. bulbelliferum Bailey
  A. cepa L. Proliferum Group*
Allium porrum L.
  A. ampeloprasum L. Porrum Group*
Allium tuberosum Rottler*
  A. odorum L.
Amaracus dictamnus Benth.
  A. tomentosus Moench
  Origanum dictamnus L.*
Anchusa
  Symphytum L.*
Anethum graveolens L.*
  Peucedanum graveolens Benth. and
    Hook.
Angelica archangelica L.*
  A. officinalis Hoffm.
Anthemis nobilis L.
  Chamaemelum nobile (L.) All.*
Armoracia lapathifolia Gilib.
  A. rusticana Gaertn., Mey., and Schreb.*
  Cochlearia armoracia L.
Asperula odorata L.
  Galium odoratum (L.) Scop.*
Brassica kaber Wheeler*
  B. arvensis Rabenh.
Chrysanthemum balsamita L.*
  Tanacetum balsamita L.
Chrysanthemum balsamita v. tanacetoides
    Hayek*
  Balsamita major Desf.
Cynoglossum
  Heliotropium L.*
Cunila origanoides Britt.*
  C. mariana L.
  Satureja origanoides L.
Dictamnus albus L.*
  D. fraxinella Pers.
Foeniculum vulgare Mill.*
  F. officinale All.
  Anethum foeniculum L.
Foeniculum vulgare v. dulce Fiori
  F. dulce Mill.
  F. vulgare v. azoricum (Mill.) Thell.*
Lavandula latifolia Medic.*
  L. spica All.

Lavandula officinalis Chaix
  L. vera DC.
  L. spica L.
  L. angustifolia Mill. subsp. angustifolia*
Levisticum officinale Koch*
  Ligusticum levisticum L.
Lippia citriodora HBK.
  Verbena triphylla L'Her.
  Aloysia triphylla Britt.*
  A. citriodora Ort.
Majorana hortensis Moench
  Origanum majorana L.*
Majorana onites Benth.
  Origanum onites L.*
Matricaria chamomilla L.
  M. recutita L.*
Mentha aquatica v. crispa Benth.*
  M. crispa L.
Mentha Citrata Ehrh.
  M. x piperita v. citrata (Ehrh.) Briq.*
Mentha Piperita L.
  M. x piperita L.*
Mentha rotundifolia Huds.
  M. spicata v. rotundifolia L.
  M. suaveolens Ehrh.*
Mentha rotundifolia v. variegata Hort.
  M. suaveolens 'Variegata'*
Mentha spicata L.*
  M. viridis L.
Nasturtium officinale R. Br.*
  N. nasturtium-aquaticum (L.) Karst.
  Rorippa nasturtium-aquaticum Hayek
Petroselinum crispum Nym.*
  P. hortense Hoffm.
  Apium petroselinum L.
  Carum petroselinum Benth. and Hook.
Phytolacca americana L.*
  P. decandra L.
Sanguisorba minor Scop.
  Pimpinella sanguisorba Gaertn.
  Poterium sanguisorba L.*
Satureja hortensis L.*
  Calamintha hortensis Hort.
Satureja montana L.*
  Calamintha montana Lam.
Tanacetum vulgare L.*
  Chrysanthemum tanacetum Karsch
  C. vulgare Bernh.
Valerianella olitoria Poll.
  V. locusta Betcke*
  V. locusta v. olitoria L.

PLATE 56. HERB SEEDS

The seeds are arranged on the plate by families which are listed below. The number preceding each family name corresponds to family number on the plate. The seeds are listed under each family by their scientific names. With a few exceptions they are in alphabetical order and are numbered to correspond with the numbers on the plate. The color of each seed is indicated after its name. An x followed by a number indicates the degree of enlargement. For example, x5 indicates that the drawing is *five times* natural size.

I Liliaceae. LILY FAMILY. x10
1. Allium porrum. Black.
2. Allium schoenoprasum. Black, somewhat glossy.

II Polygonaceae. BUCKWHEAT FAMILY. All x10
The "seeds" are the achenes, usually surrounded by the calyx valves, as shown in Plates 4, 47, and 48.
1. Rumex acetosa. Dark brown, shiny.
2. Rumex acetosella. Dark reddish brown, shiny.
3. Rumex patientia. Brown, shiny.

III Chenopodiaceae. GOOSEFOOT FAMILY
1. Atriplex hortensis. Seed enclosed. x2
2. Atriplex hortensis. Reddish brown to blackish. x5
3. Chenopodium album. Black, somewhat shiny, pericarp persistent. x14
4. Chenopodium bonus-henricus. Dull black, calyx sometimes persistent. x14

IV Phytolaccaceae. POKEWEED FAMILY
Phytolacca americana. Black, glossy. x5

V Cruciferae. MUSTARD FAMILY
Young growth of *Brassica kaber* resembles that of several other common edible mustards. The different kinds are most easily distinguished by the seeds and pods, as described below. Pods x1, seeds x10.
1. Brassica kaber (page 185). Seeds black or dark purplish-brown. The short-beaked pods spread away from the stem.
2. Raphanus raphanistrum, Wild Radish. Seeds reddish brown. The jointed pods break into short pieces, each containing one seed.
3. Brassica nigra, Black Mustard. Seeds reddish brown. The pods are short, short-beaked, and grow nearly parallel to the main stem. This species is cultivated for table mustard.
4. Sisymbrium officinale, Hedge Mustard. Seeds light brown. The small, taper-pointed pods lie flat against the main stem.
5. Brassica hirta, White Mustard. Seeds yellowish. Pods are bristly, sword-shaped, long-beaked. This species is cultivated for seeds and for greens under several variety names.

.. ..

All x10
6. Barbarea verna. Gray, sometimes with brownish mottling.
7. Barbarea vulgaris. Gray.
8. Lepidium sativum. Reddish brown.
9. Lepidium virginicum. Reddish brown.
10. Nasturtium officinale. Reddish brown.

VI Rosaceae. ROSE FAMILY
Sanguisorba minor. Light brown. x5

VII Leguminosae. PEA FAMILY
Trigonella foenum-graecum. Smooth, reddish brown. x5

VIII Rutaceae. RUE FAMILY
1. Dictamnus albus. Shiny black x5
2. Ruta graveolens. Dull black. x10

IX Umbelliferae. PARSLEY FAMILY. All x5
The mericarps or "seeds" are mostly straw-colored, the darker parts olive-brown to grayish. Numbers 3 and 11 are black.
1. Anethum graveolens.
2. Angelica archangelica.
3. Anthriscus cerefolium.
4. Carum carvi.
5. Coriandrum sativum.
6. Chaerophyllum bulbosum.
7. Cuminum cyminum.
8. Foeniculum vulgare.
9. Levisticum officinale.
10. Apium graveolens.
11. Myrrhis odorata.
12. Petroselinum crispum.
13. Pimpinella anisum.

X Boraginaceae. BORAGE FAMILY
Borago officinalis. Dark gray to black. x5

XI Labiatae. MINT FAMILY. All x10
1. Agastache foeniculum. Brown.
2. Hedeoma pulegioides. Blackish.
3. Hyssopus officinalis. Dark brown to blackish.
4. Lavandula officinalis. Dull purple-brown, shiny.
5. Majorana hortensis. Yellowish brown to reddish brown.
6. Marrubium vulgare. Dark brown to black, sometimes grayish with darker mottling.
7. Melissa officinalis. Reddish brown to blackish.
8. Mentha pulegium. Yellowish brown to reddish brown.
9. Monarda didyma. Yellowish-brown or brown.
10. Monarda fistulosa. Light brown to dark brown.
11. Monarda punctata. Grayish brown.
12. Nepeta cataria. Reddish brown to dark brown.
13. Ocimum basilicum. Dark brown to blackish.
14. Origanum vulgare. Reddish brown to dark brown.
15. Rosmarinus officinalis. Yellowish brown to dark brown.
16. Salvia officinalis. Dark brown to black.
17. Salvia sclarea. Solid brown or brown with darker veining.
18. Satureja hortensis. Medium brown streaked with dark brown.
19. Satureja montana. Light brown.
20. Thymus serpyllum. Yellowish brown to dark brown.
21. Thymus vulgaris. Reddish brown to dark brown.

XII Rubiaceae. MADDER FAMILY. x5
Asperula odorata. Grayish, with spinelike hairs.

XIII Valerianaceae. VALERIAN FAMILY. x5
Valerianella olitoria. Rough, grayish. This is the fruit. A seed develops in only one of the three cells.

XIV Compositae. COMPOSITE FAMILY
All x10 except number 3.
These are the achenes or fruits. Each contains one seed.
1. Anthemis nobilis. Grayish brown with light ribs.
2. Artemisia absinthium. Light brown.
3. Carthamus tinctorius. White, smooth. x5
4. Cichorium intybus. Straw colored to brown, sometimes mottled.
5. Matricaria chamomilla. Grayish brown, prominent white ribs.
6. Tanacetum vulgare. Brownish.

PLATE 56.

I Liliaceae. LILY FAMILY

II Polygonaceae. BUCKWHEAT FAMILY.

III Chenopodiaceae

1   2

1   2   3

1

3

VII Leguminosae. PEA FAMILY

VIII Rutaceae. RUE FAMILY

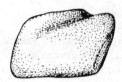

1   2

X Boraginaceae.
BORAGE FAMILY

IX Umbelliferae. PARSLEY FAMILY

XI Labiatae.

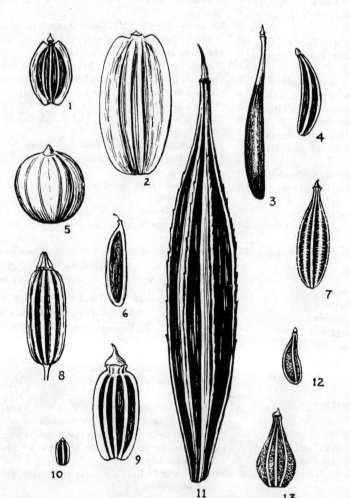

1   2   8   3

7   7   9   10

15   16

20

HERB SEEDS

GOOSEFOOT FAMILY

2

4

IV Phytolaccaceae.
POKEWEED FAMILY

V Cruciferae. MUSTARD FAMILY

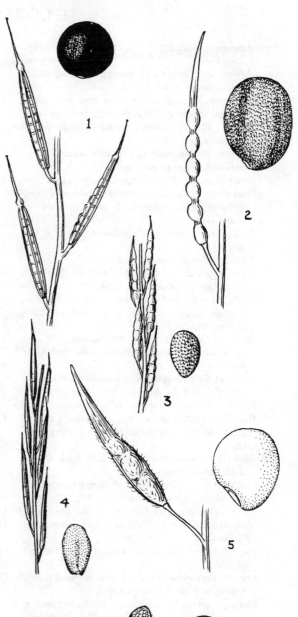

1

2

3

4

5

VI Rosaceae. ROSE FAMILY

XII Rubiaceae. MADDER FAMILY

XIII Valerianaceae.
VALERIAN FAMILY

MINT FAMILY

4

5

6

14

11   12   13

6   7   10   8   9

17

18   19

21

XIV Compositae. COMPOSITE FAMILY

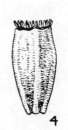

1   2

3

4

5   6

GLOSSARY

Achene. Small, dry, hard, one-seeded, indehiscent fruit.

Acuminate. Gradually tapering to a long point.

Acute. Sharp-pointed.

Alternate. Having one leaf or bud at a node; placed singly at different heights on stem.

Annual. Of one season's duration from seed to maturity and death.

Anther. Pollen-bearing part of stamen.

Apetalous. Having no petals.

Auriculate. With ear-shaped appendages.

Awl-shaped. Narrow and sharp-pointed; gradually tapering from the base to a slender or stiff point.

Axil. The upper angle formed where a leaf joins a stem.

Axillary. Situated in an axil.

Axis. The main or central line of development of a plant or organ; the stem.

Beak. A long, prominent, and substantial point. Usually applied to prolongations of fruits and pistils.

Berry. A fleshy fruit, soft throughout.

Bi-. A Latin prefix signifying two, twice, or doubly.

Biennial. Of two seasons' duration from seed to maturity and death.

Blade. The expanded part of a leaf.

Bract. A much-reduced leaf, particularly one of the small or scalelike leaves of a flower cluster.

Bulb. An underground leaf bud with fleshy scales and a short axis.

Calyx. The outer whorl of floral envelopes; the outer perianth whorl.

Calyx valve. In Rumex, one of the enlarged, mature sepals which adhere to and surround the achene.

Capsule. Dry, dehiscent fruit of a compound pistil.

Carpel. One of the units of a compound pistil. A simple pistil has one carpel.

Chaff. A small, thin scale or bract, becoming dry or membranous; in particular the bracts in the flower heads of the Composite Family.

Ciliate. Fringed with hairs on the margin.

Clasping. Of leaves, partly or completely surrounding a stem.

Cleft. Lobed, with the incisions extending halfway or more to the midrib of a leaf.

Clove. One of the divisions of a compound bulb.

Compound bulb. Separating into cloves or bulblets.

Compound leaf. A leaf in which the blade consists of two or more separate parts (leaflets).

Compound pistil. A pistil composed of two or more fused carpels.

Confluent. Running into each other. Blending together.

Cordate. Heart-shaped, with the point away from the base.

Corm. A solid, bulblike part usually underground; the enlarged, fleshy, solid base of a stem.

Corolla. The inner whorl of floral envelopes; the inner perianth whorl.

Corymb. A flat or convex flower cluster with the outer flower opening first.

Creeping. Running along the ground and rooting its entire length, as of stems.

Crenate. With rounded teeth; scalloped.

Crown. An inner appendage to a petal or to the throat of a corolla.

Cuneate. Wedge-shaped; triangular with the acute angle downward.

Cyme. A broad, more or less flat-topped flower cluster, with central flowers opening first.

Decompound. More than once compound or divided.

Decumbent. Reclining at base but the summit ascending.

Dehiscent. Opening regularly by valves or slits, as a capsule.

Dentate. Toothed, with teeth pointing out.

Dichotomous. Forking regularly by pairs.

Dioecious. With staminate and pistillate flowers each on different plants.

Disk. A receptacle in the heads of the Composite Family.

Disk flowers. The tubular flowers in the center of the heads of the Composite Family as distinguished from the marginal or ray flowers.

Dissected. Divided into many slender segments.

Elliptical. Having the shape of an ellipse; oval or oblong with the ends rounded.

Entire. Having an even margin; not toothed, notched, or divided.

Exserted. Projecting beyond an envelope.

Fertile. Of stamens, bearing pollen; of flowers, bearing seeds.

Filament. The part of the stamen which supports the anther.

Filiform. Threadlike; long and very slender.

Fruit. The ripened ovary. The seed-bearing organ.

Gamopetalous. Having the petals united; having a corolla of one piece.

Glabrous. Without hairs.

Gland. A secreting part or appendage. The term is often used for small swellings or projections on various organs.

Glandular. Furnished with glands; glandlike.

Glaucous. Covered or whitened with a bloom.

Globose. Spherical in form or nearly so.

Habit. The general aspect of a plant or its mode of growth.

Habitat. The home of a plant; the situation in which a plant grows wild.

Halberd-shaped, hastate. Shaped like an arrowhead but with basal lobes pointing outward.

Head. A short, compact flower cluster of more or less sessile flowers.

Herbaceous. Not woody.

Hispid. Provided with stiff or bristly hairs.

Imbricated. Overlapping like shingles on a roof.

Incised. Cut sharply and irregularly.

Indehiscent. Not regularly opening, as a seed pod or anther.

Indigenous. Native and original to a region.

Inferior ovary. An ovary in which the sepals appear attached to the top.

Inflorescence. A flower cluster; a mode of flower-bearing.

Involucre. A whorl of small leaves or bracts standing close below a flower or flower cluster.

Irregular flower. A flower having parts of a whorl or series not all alike.

Keeled. Ridged like the bottom of a boat.

Lacerate. With the margin appearing as if torn.

Lanceolate. Several time longer than wide, broadest near the base and narrowed to tip.

Lateral. On or at the side.

Leaflet. One part of a compound leaf.

Ligulate. Strap-shaped. Used particularly of the ray flowers of the Composite Family.

Linear. Long and narrow, parallel margins.

Lobed. Divided into segments toward middle.

Locule. The cavity of an ovary or anther.

Loculicidal dehiscence. Splitting through the back of each cell or carpel of a capsule.

Mericarp. One of the two carpels of the fruit of a member of the Parsley Family.

-Merous. Referring to the number of parts; as flowers 5-merous, in which the parts of each kind or series are five or in fives.

Monoecious. Having separate staminate and pistillate flowers on the same plant.

Node. A joint or place where leaves are attached to a stem or branch.

Ob-. A Latin syllable usually indicating inversion; as *obovate*, inverted ovate.

Oblanceolate. Lanceolate but with the narrow end towards the stem.

Oblong. Longer than broad and with the sides nearly parallel most of their length.

Obtuse. Blunt or rounded at the end.

Opposite. Having two leaves or buds at the node.

Orbicular. Circular.

Ovary. The part of the pistil bearing ovules.

Ovate. With an outline like that of a hen's egg, with the broad end toward the base.

Panicle. An elongated, irregularly branched, raceme-like inflorescence.

Paniculate. Resembling a panicle.

Papilionaceous. Having a standard, wings, and keel, like a pea or bean flower.

Pappus. The modified calyx limb of the Composite Family, forming a crown of bristles, scales, etc., at the summit of the achene.

Pectinate. Comblike; pinnatifid with very narrow close divisions or parts.

Pedicel. The stem of an individual flower in a cluster.

Peduncle. The stem of a solitary flower or of a flower cluster.

Perennial. Of three or more seasons' duration.

Perfect flower. A flower having both stamens and pistil.

Perianth. The floral envelope considered together. Used mostly for flowers having no clear distinction between calyx and corolla, as in the Lily Family.

Pericarp. The matured ovary.

Persistent. Remaining attached; of leaves, not falling at the same time.

Petal. One of the divisions of the corolla.

Petiole. The stalk of a leaf.

Pinnate. Feather-formed.

Pinnately compound. With the leaflets arranged on each side of a common axis of a compound leaf.

Pistil. The ovule-bearing and seed-bearing organ with style and stigma.

Pistillate. Having pistils and no stamens.

Pod. A general term to designate a dry, dehiscent fruit.

Pollen. The spores or grains borne by the anther which contain the male element.

Pubescent. Covered with soft, short hairs.

Raceme. A simple flower cluster of pediceled flowers on a common elongated axis.

Radical. Of leaves, appearing to come from the root or from the base of the stem near the ground.

Ray flower. One of the modified flowers of the outer part of the heads of some of the Composite Family, with a straplike extension of the corolla.

Receptacle. The more or less enlarged or elongated end of the axis which bears the collected flowers of a head.

Recurved. Curved outward or backward.

Reflexed. Bent abruptly outward or backward.

Regular flower. A flower having all the parts of a whorl or series alike.

Revolute. Having margins rolled backward or under.

Rhizome. An underground stem; a rootstock.

Rootstock. An underground stem; a rhizome.

Rosette. A dense cluster of leaves borne on a very short stem or axis.

Rugose. Wrinkled; generally because of the depressions of the veins in the upper surface of the leaf.

Runcinate. Sharply incised, the segments directed backward.

Runner. A slender, trailing stem taking root at at the nodes.

Sagittate. Shaped like an arrowhead; triangular with the basal lobes pointing downward.

Scape. A leafless flowering stem arising from the ground.

Schizocarp. A pericarp which splits into one-seeded portions.

Sepal. One of the divisions of the calyx.

Serrate. Having sharp teeth pointing forward.

Serrulate Finely serrate.

Sessile. Without a stalk.

Sheath. A long, more or less tubular structure surrounding an organ or part.

Simple bulb. Not separating into cloves or bulblets.

Simple leaf. A leaf in which the blade is all in one piece.

Sinuate. Wavy-margined.

Spathe. The bract or leaf surrounding or subtending a flower cluster.

Spatulate. Gradually narrowed downward from a rounded summit.

Spike. A flower cluster with sessile or nearly sessile flowers borne on a common elongated axis.

Spinose. Having spines.

Stamen. The pollen-bearing or male organ of a flower.

Staminate. Having stamens and no pistils.

Sterile. Of plants, flowers, or stamens, infertile, barren.

Stigma. The part of the pistil which receives the pollen.

Stipule. A basal appendage of a petiole, usually one of two.

Stolon. A shoot that bends to the ground, taking root at its tip and thus giving rise to a new plant.

Stoloniferous. Bearing runners or shoots that take root.

Striate. Marked with fine longitudinal lines or ridges.

Style. The part of the pistil connecting the ovary and stigma, usually more or less elongated.

Succulent. Juicy; fleshy; soft and thickened in texture.

Taproot. A main root with a stout body, usually vertical.

Terminal. At the end of a stem or branch.

Ternate. In threes.

Throat. The opening of a gamopetalous corolla or gamopetalous calyx.

Trifoliate. Of three leaflets.

Tubercle. In Rumex, the protuberance at the base of the enlarged midrib of the calyx valve.

Umbel. An umbrella-like flower cluster.

Umbellet. A secondary umbel.

Valve. One of the units or pieces into which a capsule splits; a separable part of a pod.

Viscid. Sticky.

Whorl. An arrangement of leaves, petals, or other parts in a circle around an axis.

Whorled. Having leaves or buds arranged in a group of three or more at a node.

Woolly. Provided with long, soft, more or less matted hairs.

INDEX

211